Tales from

Dog River

Tales from Dog River

The Complete *Corner Gas* Guide

Michele Sponagle

with a Foreword by Brent Butt

PENGUIN
CANADA

PENGUIN CANADA

Published by the Penguin Group

Penguin Group (Canada), 90 Eglinton Avenue East, Suite 700, Toronto, Ontario, Canada M4P 2Y3
(a division of Pearson Canada Inc.)

Penguin Group (USA) Inc., 375 Hudson Street, New York, New York 10014, U.S.A.
Penguin Books Ltd, 80 Strand, London WC2R 0RL, England
Penguin Ireland, 25 St Stephen's Green, Dublin 2, Ireland (a division of Penguin Books Ltd)
Penguin Group (Australia), 250 Camberwell Road, Camberwell, Victoria 3124, Australia
(a division of Pearson Australia Group Pty Ltd)
Penguin Books India Pvt Ltd, 11 Community Centre, Panchsheel Park, New Delhi – 110 017, India
Penguin Group (NZ), cnr Airborne and Rosedale Roads, Albany, Auckland 1310, New Zealand
(a division of Pearson New Zealand Ltd)
Penguin Books (South Africa) (Pty) Ltd, 24 Sturdee Avenue, Rosebank, Johannesburg 2196, South Africa

Penguin Books Ltd, Registered Offices: 80 Strand, London WC2R 0RL, England

First published 2006

(QUE) 10 9 8 7 6 5 4 3 2

Manufactured in the USA.

Library and Archives Canada Cataloguing in Publication data available upon request.

ISBN-10: 0-14-305031-1

ISBN-13: 978-0-14-305031-5

Visit the Penguin Group (Canada) website at **www.penguin.ca**

Visit the official *Corner Gas* website at **www.cornergas.com**

Special and corporate bulk purchase rates available; please see
www.penguin.ca/corporatesales or call 1-800-810-3104 ext. 477 or 474

For my parents, Mervin

(from Avonport, Nova Scotia, population 302)

and Marion

(born in Willingdon, Alberta, population 287),

who taught me to truly appreciate small-town humour

CORNER GAS

Contents

PREMIER OF SASKATCHEWAN

LEGISLATIVE BUILDING
REGINA, CANADA S4S 0B3

A Message from the Premier of Saskatchewan

On behalf of the Government of Saskatchewan, I am pleased to welcome Corner Gas *fans to the companion guide to this popular show.*

Since 2004, the folks from Dog River have been entertaining Canadians with the only primetime series set and filmed completely in Saskatchewan. Corner Gas *has provided not only employment and economic benefits to Saskatchewan people, but also raised the profile of our province.*

In Canada, Saskatchewan has often been regarded as the place where "there's not a lot goin' on." But, as the lyrics say, "Look closer, baby, you're so wrong." Our film industry is rapidly expanding, and our government was pleased to give it a boost by providing tax breaks and financing for the Canada/Saskatchewan Production Studios.

Many talented people call Saskatchewan home, and we are particularly proud that three of the series' stars, Brent Butt, Eric Peterson, and Janet Wright, are Saskatchewan natives. As well, the series attracts many well-known guest stars, and even gave me the chance to make my acting debut!

I commend CTV, Penguin Canada, and the author for producing this guide. I invite everyone to Saskatchewan to tour the town of Rouleau (Dog River), and I hope that you will continue to tune in to the antics of Brent, Lacey, Wanda, Hank, Emma, Oscar, Davis, and Karen and their friends and neighbours in Dog River, Saskatchewan.

Lorne Calvert
Premier

Saskatchewan Centennial 2005™

Foreword

By Brent Butt

IN MANY WAYS it was a night like any other night—dark, cold, and full of numbing silence. When I began to hear the footsteps, they echoed against the wet stone walls. I crouched low behind the dumpster, took a deep breath, and steeled my nerves. This time I had the jump on Rico, but he was still a dangerous son of a badger.

Wait. I'm sorry. That's the start to my action-thriller-mystery-suspense-romance-detective novel, the working title of which is *Low Behind the Dumpster*. This should be the foreword to the *Corner Gas* book. So here goes.

I was pleased as a pumpkin to see this book come together. It was the culmination of a lot of hard work. Not mine, of course, but other people worked very hard I'm sure. I mean, just look at it. It's full of words and pictures and everything. This stuff doesn't just get magically spun into existence by bearded elves as we slumber. Someone has to do a lot of work. While we slumber. And I, for one, appreciate it.

The cast and I, as well as producers and crew and TV executives, were all interviewed (mercilessly grilled, if you want the truth) in an attempt to shed a little light on the behind-the-scenes workings of life in Dog River. Those questions caused me to reflect back on the heady days of yesteryear and to glean through the images and memories in my mind's eye. The sum of which is to say, this has been an incredible ride.

You can't even imagine the number of laughs I've had over the past five or six years. Honestly—it's ridiculous to have this much fun. Someone with more integrity would be ashamed to have this much fun. But I can't help it. I have loved television since I was a kid, and I still love it, and to be blessed with the opportunity to follow my dreams and wade around neck-deep in the process of making television is more than I could have asked for. And yet I did ask for it. For some crazy reason CTV said "Okay," and for that (and for so much more), I will be forever grateful. CTV is a strange entity. It's a television network run by people who actually enjoy television. Wrap your head around that one.

As much as anything, this experience has been about relationships. Working with my partners David Storey and Virginia Thompson has been like working with smooth peanut butter and sweet, sweet jam, that is, if I represent a piece of bread ... or toast ... okay, that analogy isn't working. My point is this: David Storey and Virginia Thompson have become, quite simply, two of my favourite people on the planet. They are kind, generous, intelligent, and professional. They're also big laughers, which is great for my ego. I couldn't imagine having done this without them. I'm certainly glad I didn't try.

Also, a few words about the cast. It has been gob-droppingly awesome watching this incredible group of actors breathe life into the people on the page. I marvel at

their abilities every day and am so very grateful for their vision and their talent. Can you even imagine anyone else in these roles? Vincent Gardenia as Brent perhaps, but the rest of them—forget it.

I'd like to mention the writers. They are all tremendous typers, or "typists" as they insist on being called. Many, many words per minute. Aside from their dexterity, they are also a wonderfully savvy pack of eggheads who can twist a story out of nothing and pound almost any predicament into a solution. People often say to me, "How can you guys keep making the show so funny?" The truth is, the funny is the easy part. Jokes and comical dialogue flow like tap water in the writers' room. The question should be, "How do you guys keep making stories that have a beginning, middle, and end and that make some kind of sense?" Because therein lies the lifting. To watch these writers solve story problems or create resolutions is humbling. I bet they're good at chess, too.

Lastly, I want to mention the crew on our show: the men and women who show up for work at insane hours of the morning and stay until insane hours of the evening, all the while going about their business (rain, cold, hail, bugs, coyotes, you-name-it) with the most incredible combination of wit and grit that I've ever seen. If I were held hostage by an evil group of killers, I would rather see this crew coming to my rescue than a band of marines. I also like to think that maybe they would come to my rescue. Fingers crossed.

I have to sign off now. We're shooting as I write this. The camera is ready and they're calling for me on set. It dawns on me that I haven't even looked at my lines yet. Oops. Looks like Rico has his revenge at last. Curse you, Rico.

DOG RIVER
DOG RIVER

Welcome to Dog River

Welcome to Dog River, the place where you'll find some pretty interesting folks—Brent, Emma, Oscar, Lacey, Wanda, Karen, Davis, and Hank. You probably know them. What you might not know is the story of how they leapt from the comedic brain of Brent Butt and landed on your television screen.

To turn ideas into fully formed episodes, a plethora of talented folks—from writers and electricians to editors and cast—rally together. What you see on television is just the tip of the proverbial iceberg. There's a complex, fascinating underbelly to *Corner Gas,* a world where, despite what the lyrics to the opening song claim, there really is a heck of a lot going on.

Let's rewind to the very beginning of the *Corner Gas* story, to where a guy from small-town Saskatchewan wanted to make people laugh.

Oh Baby:
The Birth of a TV Show

IN THE WORLD of Canadian television, *Corner Gas* is a bit of circus freak, a true anomaly. New, freshly hatched television shows have as much chance for long-term survival as a minority government. The odds are stacked against them even getting off the ground. The landscape of Canadian TV is littered with dead shows, roadkill created by a lack of funds and a lack of viewers. *Corner Gas* beat the CanTV hex. It has succeeded in a big way, unrivalled and unmatched by anything that has come before it. It has broken new ground in television and has prompted many people to think that the phrase "Canadian-made hit" is not an oxymoron.

Remember the episode in which Hank believes he's psychic? Not even his soothsaying powers could have foreseen how huge *Corner Gas* would become, beating well-entrenched ratings winners like *Friends* and *Hockey Night in Canada* in its inaugural year and spiking to almost 3 million viewers during the Season 3 episode Merry Gasmas. It is official. *Corner Gas* is a hit.

But *Corner Gas* might have become just another pipe dream if it hadn't been for Brent Butt, his producing partners, and a gang of cheerleaders at CTV, the network that broadcasts the show across Canada and the one that came up with the cash to produce it. The idea for a comedy set in small-town Saskatchewan, featuring a cast of eight characters who didn't really have a lot going on, could have stayed stuck forever in that deep pothole on Main Street in Dog River if it hadn't been for a film script that didn't fly.

Brent Butt has spent his life criss-crossing Canada to perform his stand-up comedy act in venues small and large. He's eaten a lot of chili cheese dogs, watched drunks being tossed out of bars, and lived out of a suitcase, all the time sharpening his laid-back conversational brand of comedy, something he calls "coffee shop humour." Whether commenting on finding a wayward pair of underwear on the street or making cracks about what you might overhear in a small town ("Excuse me, sir. Will you hold my baby while I count this cash?"), Brent honed in on everyday stuff we could all relate to. His humour was based on the philosophy that people are more alike than they are different, and he relayed it with easygoing wit.

With those basic principles floating around in his brain, Brent started to write a script that he hoped could become a feature film. And since it didn't matter particularly where it took place, he set his story in Saskatchewan, where he was born and raised. Writing what you know is always a smart way to go. But Brent wasn't entirely happy with what he wrote. He scrapped the movie script, then began to noodle around the idea of retooling it into a premise for a TV show. "I am not terribly ambitious," says Brent modestly. "After I wrote that, I didn't do anything with it."

Nothing, that is, until his friend David Storey phoned him. The director had landed a pitch session with Brent Haynes at CTV. David had bumped into Haynes at the 2002 Gemini Awards, and Haynes had said he would be interested in a western-based comedy. David and Brent met at Bojangles in downtown Vancouver to brainstorm ideas. It was then that Brent revealed for the first time his idea for something called *Corner Gas*. A few months after talking to Haynes at the Gemini Awards night, David headed to Toronto for a meeting with him, armed with four concepts for possible shows. The last one David presented was for *Corner Gas*.

"David pulled out this crumpled-up, single sheet of paper with the words *Corner Gas* on it," Haynes recalls. "I said sure. Not so much because of this particular project, but because I really wanted to work with Brent, who I knew from my time at CBC, when he was doing *Bedtime with Brent Butt*. I always loved Brent's stuff and had seen him perform at the Just for Laughs festival in Montreal."

Ed Robinson, senior vice-president, comedy and variety programming, CTV, feels the same way about Brent's talent. "I like his approach to comedy," says Ed. "He has a touch of the Everyman quality to him, and his jokes are something that we can all understand and relate to." As well, there also happened to be $240 million sitting in a bank account, earmarked for developing television projects for CTV over a period of seven years. "Having that money already in hand gave us the chance to deal with creative issues first and foremost," explains Ed. "Usually you're spending a good chunk of time waiting for your financing to come through. With *Corner Gas* and other series, we were able to make them happen much more quickly."

The Players

Brent Butt, creator and executive producer

David Storey, executive producer and director

Virginia Thompson, executive producer

Ivan Fecan, president and CEO of Bell Globemedia; CEO, CTV Inc.

Susanne Boyce, president, CTV programming and chair of the CTV media group

Ed Robinson, senior vice-president, comedy and variety programming, CTV

Brent Haynes, director of programming for The Comedy Network

Louise Clark, director, western independent production, CTV

The combination of ready cash and the availability of Canada's hottest stand-up comic set the scene for fast-tracked series development.

Around the same time, Haynes was in a meeting with top gun Susanne Boyce, CTV's resident Wonder Woman. As president of CTV programming, she has played a giant part in the revitalization of CTV, turning it into the number one network in Canada. She has always pushed the creative minds she works with to think big. "Off the cuff, kind of jokingly, Susanne asked me, 'What's your dream project? If you could do anything, what would it be? Name it right now,'" remembers Haynes. "I told her that I would do a show with Brent Butt, with David Storey as director and Mark Farrell writing. 'Okay, then,' she said. She dared me to go and put the team together. I went back to the piece of paper that had *Corner Gas* written on it and I started calling everyone to see if they would be willing to develop it into a series. They all said yes. I also phoned Louise Clark, CTV's director of western independent production, and said, 'I'm in way over my head. Can you help me?'"

If the CTV execs liked the scripts, *Corner Gas* could become a reality. If they didn't, the show could wind up joining the oodles of other fledging TV shows that met with a quick end.

When a television series has been given the go-ahead to move into development, issues like budgets, who will be working on the series, where it is going to be shot, and what exactly the show is going to be about need to be hashed out. Moving ahead with *Corner Gas* meant determining all those things, and producing a couple of scripts. From there, CTV would decide whether it was good enough to take it to the next stage—a gigantic, and expensive, step that involves hiring a cast and crew, and building sets for the creation of an episode.

When Louise entered the picture, one of the first things she did was try to find the missing pieces in the team that could bring *Corner Gas* to life. A writer was still needed, someone Brent Butt could work with closely, someone in the same league as him. CTV had an idea of who it should be. Brent and David had someone in mind, too. Would there be a showdown between the two sides? Peace prevailed. The man everyone wanted was Mark Farrell, a veteran comedy writer who works as a producer on *This Hour Has 22 Minutes* and, in the past, *Made in Canada*. Today, each side lets the other think that it was its idea to get Mark involved. We're not saying a word ...

The initial call to Mark, living in Halifax, came from David Storey. "He and Brent had this idea for a show that was based on the life Brent might have had if he didn't go into stand-up comedy," says Mark. "It seemed to click, and I thought it could work because it was different from anything else on television then. The next thing I knew, I had a plane ticket for Vancouver and found myself in a meeting with Brent Haynes, Brent Butt, Louise, and David."

In that meeting, the concept for *Corner Gas* was fine-tuned further. Although the idea at first was for there to be more than the eight lead characters the show has now, these had been cut back to seven at one point, then boosted up to eight. Brent had originally thought that he'd only have a father on the show. The backstory was that his mother had died. He eventually decided he didn't want that and added the character of Emma.

It was time to work on possible storylines and characters—something you've got to do before plunging into the script-writing stage. Brent, David, and Mark checked into the Holiday Inn in Vancouver to nail down the details. After five days and late nights, fuelled by coffee, junk food, and cheap meals at the late-night eatery Denny's, they came up with a template for *Corner Gas*. Then Mark and Brent each wrote a script, trading them off to one another for tweaks and rewrites, a creative spit and polish.

Scripts for two episodes, Ruby Reborn and Tax Man, emerged. Off they went to the execs at CTV. If they liked the scripts, *Corner Gas* could become a reality. If they didn't, the show could wind up on a dead-end street, joining the oodles of other fledgling Canadian television shows that met with a quick end.

The last bit of business to take care of before production on the first pair of

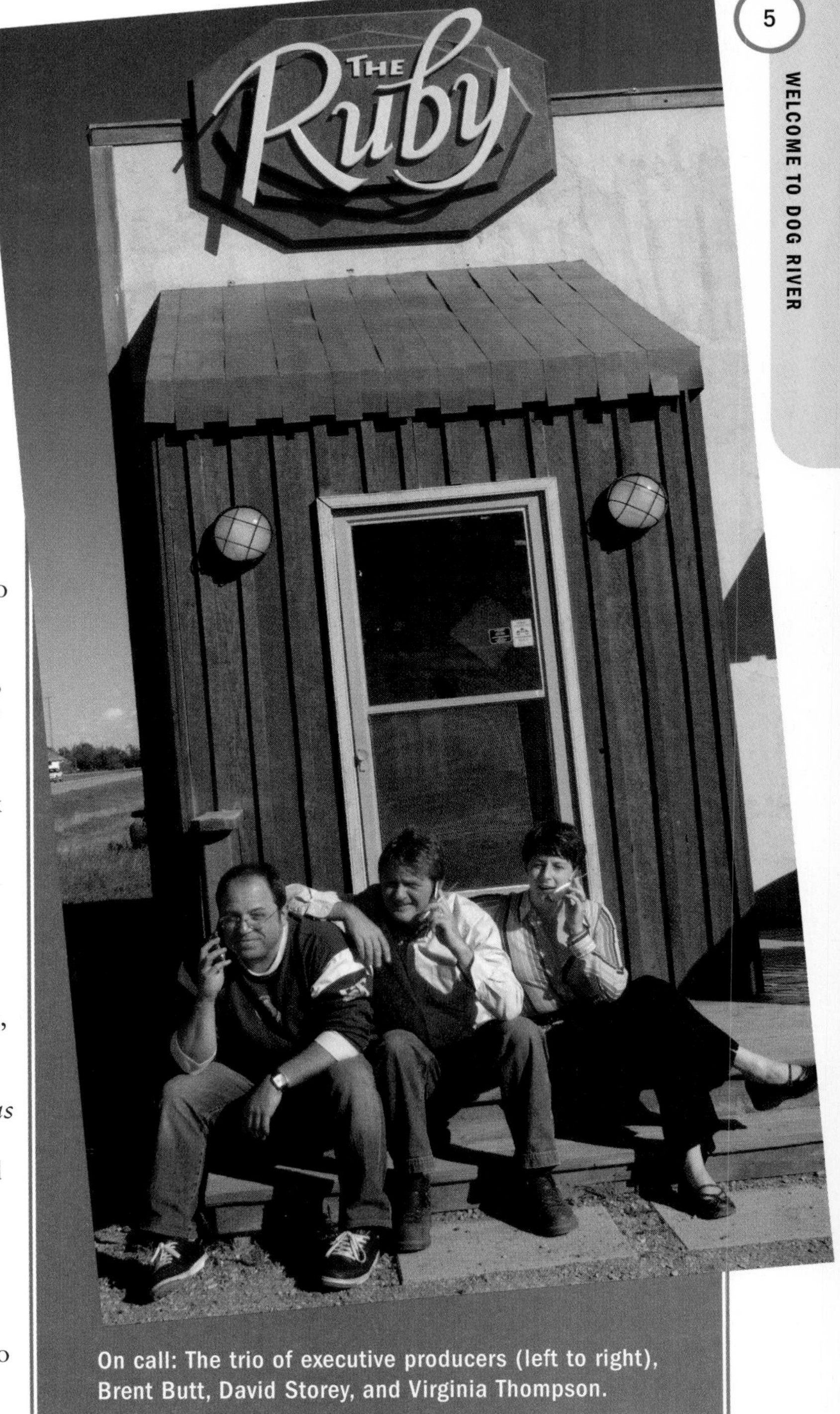

On call: The trio of executive producers (left to right), Brent Butt, David Storey, and Virginia Thompson.

episodes could start was to find a third executive producer, to work with Brent and David. Brent was the comedic brain. David was the directing guru. Louise Clark needed someone who had experience producing episodic television. Enter, stage left, Virginia Thompson from Vérité Films, the company behind the internationally successful *Incredible Story Studio,* a youth-targeted TV show, and *renegadepress.com,* a drama series for teens. Louise knew that Virginia had the business and creative smarts that would complement the skills of David and Brent.

Virginia had never met either of her future co–executive producers. David called her to say that he and Brent were putting together a comedy series called *Corner Gas*. She wasn't sure it was right for her. When she heard "Canadian" and "comedy," she assumed it was a sketch-based show rather than a scripted sitcom. But when she received the scripts that Mark and Brent had written, she became pumped. "I was blown away by the material," says Virginia. "I knew that I could contribute."

The trio met in Regina in November 2002. Virginia took a motherly approach, urging David and Brent to take their time in putting together the right team. "I gave them lots of advice. I told them that they had to really figure out who their partners should be. It's like a marriage and it's difficult to get out. A stormy relationship will impact the show. You don't want anything to affect it negatively."

And so Virginia joined the all-boys' club. She and her producing partner Robert de Lint moved out of their basement office and into a spacious downtown Regina office building. The threesome of Brent, Virginia, and David then formed a production company, which they called Prairie Pants Productions, and waited, with bated breath, for feedback from CTV on the scripts.

The scripts were on the desk of Brent Haynes. "When I read them, I was laughing out loud. They were really, really funny," he says. But since CTV was the one that would be coming up with most of the cash to make *Corner Gas,* it had to have the blessing of its key players at the network, including Ivan Fecan, Bell Globemedia and CTV Inc.'s head honcho.

Fortunately, Ivan was a believer in Brent Butt's ability to carry a series. "Anyone who is a fan of stand-up comedy has seen Brent in the clubs or on stand-up specials like The Comedy Network's *Comedy Now!* He's someone who instantaneously connects with an audience," Ivan explains. "I think everyone feels they know Brent—or somebody just like him. With his laid back, sardonic Canadian wit, he's a natural fit for a Canadian sitcom."

"The scripts were very smart and had a sensibility that reminded me of *Newhart,*" Susanne recalls. "A lot of passion went into the writing and it showed in every line." She knew the concept for *Corner Gas* was solid and that the creative team had engaging storylines in mind, but she had concerns about whether the laughs would get lost in the translation from idea to script. "I loved the outline for Tax Man," she says, "but I wondered if it could get off the page."

Proof that those doubts had been put aside came after an industry event in Winnipeg as Louise and Brent Haynes sat in a bar at The Fort Garry hotel. They discussed whether their bosses at the network would give the okay to make *Corner Gas.* "I remember that our waiter had on a name tag that said *Brent,*" remembers Louise. "We thought that was a good sign, then Brent's cell phone rang. It was Ed. He gave us the official go-ahead.

Brent and I screamed like little girls. We were going to have the chance to make 13 episodes of *Corner Gas*!"

They phoned David and Virginia to give them the good news, but had trouble locating Brent Butt. Finally, David got hold of him. Their conversation went something like this:

David: "The network has ordered the series."

Brent: "What do you mean?"

David: "It's official. We're going into production."

Brent: "What do you mean?"

It took a few minutes for Brent to fully grasp what it all really did mean. His idea for a comedy about a guy working at a small-town gas station was going to become a reality.

With the writing and producing players in place, CTV and the producers of the show could start with finding seven actors for each of the key roles—Lacey, Wanda, Hank, Oscar, Karen, Davis, and Emma. Brent, of course, had already secured his part as leading man. When it came time for casting, there was spirited discussion as to what kind of talent was needed for the show. Was it comics or thespians that would work best? Both approaches had their strong supporters. Brent Haynes, with his strong background from The Comedy Network, felt that stand-up comics should be hired. Louise Clark, who has a background in the development of dramas, instinctively favoured a cast that had drama experience. To break the stalemate, Ivan Fecan weighed in with his opinion. He felt actors were needed to play off the funny. For the role of Lacey, for example, he suggested that a knock-out dramatic actress who could play straight to Brent's jokes was the way to go. This marked a turning point in the creative process in terms of what kind of actors the producers sought to become part of the *Corner Gas* cast.

Finding the right talent was time-consuming. The producers travelled across Canada five times, holding auditions from Regina to Vancouver, and in Toronto. Eventually they found their magnificent seven: Lorne Cardinal (Davis Quinton), Fred Ewanuick (Hank Yarbo), Nancy Robertson (Wanda Dollard), Tara Spencer-Nairn (Karen Pelly), Janet Wright (Emma Leroy), Eric Peterson (Oscar Leroy), and Gabrielle Miller (Lacey Burrows). Now, the search was on for the perfect place that could be transformed into Dog River.

Lunch bunch: The *Corner Gas* cast is made up of outstanding actors.

Rolling in Rouleau

SINCE THE BEGINNING, when *Corner Gas* was a wee seed of an idea, Brent Butt had a vision of shooting this new weekly television series in Saskatchewan. Such a thing had never been done. The centres of the universe for Canadian television production have always been Toronto and Vancouver. Perhaps it was time for Saskatchewan, the skinny rectangular-ish province in the middle of the country, to get a piece of the action. But it's not that simple. You have to have the resources, everything from access to camera equipment to post-production facilities, close at hand.

Up until this point, things were moving along as smooth as butter in getting *Corner Gas* on the air. Now Brent prepared to do battle with the networks about producing the series in his hometown

province. He had a prepared speech ready to unleash, including, if needed, a because-I-said-so. He would do whatever it took, including arm wrestling with Louise and Brent Haynes, to make sure the show would be both set and shot in Saskatchewan. A simple "yes, of course" from the network right off the bat extinguished the need for Brent to launch into his carefully crafted list of arguments in favour of filming there. He was almost disappointed not to be able to use them.

Everyone agreed with Brent. The series would be created entirely in Saskatchewan. Most of the interior shots (with the exception of those taking place in and around the Corner Gas station) would be done in Regina, at the new Canada Saskatchewan Production Studios, opened in 2002. It had over 3250 square metres of studio space. The exterior shots were a whole other matter. The crew needed a small town where there was room to build sets for The Ruby diner and the gas station, and space for the glut of trucks, trailers, and equipment that comes with shooting a series this big.

Brent had a mental picture of what he wanted. His Dog River had to be nice, but not too nice ("the kind of place where you

Extreme makeover: Before and after—the site of *Corner Gas* in Rouleau as dirt-covered field (above) and slick set (below).

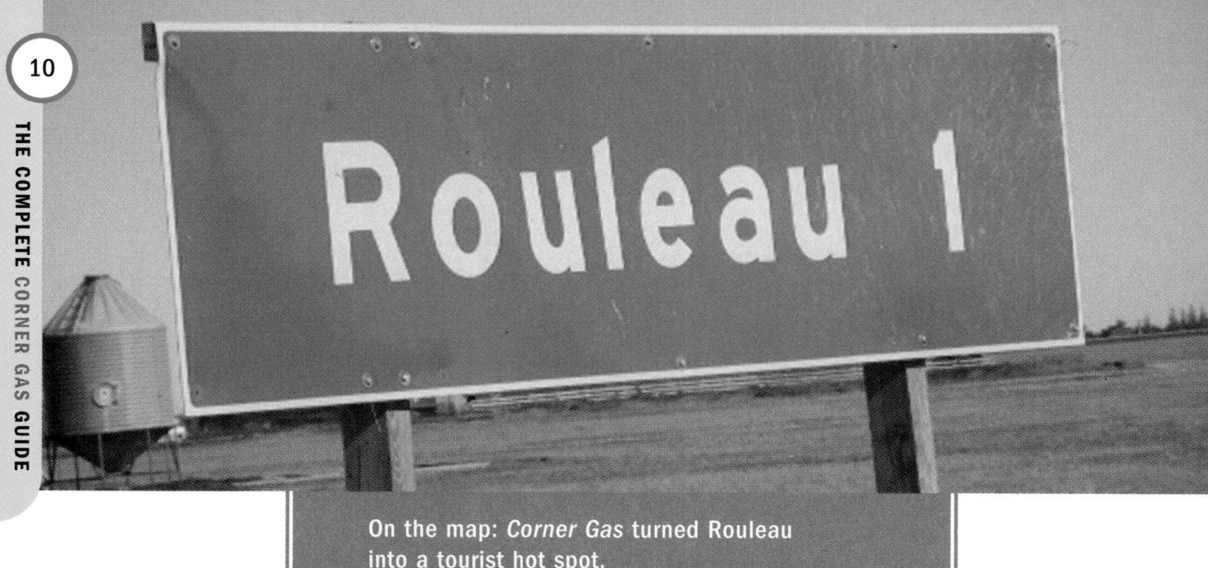

On the map: *Corner Gas* turned Rouleau into a tourist hot spot.

might find half a pickup truck in the yard"), flat—really flat—and close to Regina. Virginia, David, the pair of Brents, production designer Hugh Shankland, CTV's Louise Clark, and location manager Bill Sorochan piled into a minivan and took to the road to find *the* corner for *Corner Gas*.

Over the course of three weeks, small towns across Saskatchewan were scrutinized—about 15 in total. As the group discussed the pros and cons of each contender, Brent Butt would be quiet, then pipe up, "Not flat enough." "What about this place?" Once again, not flat enough.

Approaching Rouleau, population five hundred and about 45 minutes from Regina, you could almost hear the tires squeal as someone yelled, "Stop!" There it was: a vacant chunk of land fronted by a perfect X, formed by the intersection of two dirt roads. It matched perfectly with what Brent imagined to be the ideal corner for Corner Gas. From that spot, the tops of the buildings along Main Street could be seen. Across the road was an old wooden grain elevator—a rare sight these days in rural Saskatchewan. And not a hill, grassy knoll, slope, mound, dip, or elevation to be seen. It was undeniably flat. There you could watch your dog run away for three days, as the old prairie joke goes. Brent was happy.

In just four weeks, The Ruby and Corner Gas went from being concepts on paper to finished buildings. The gas station looked undeniably authentic—so much so that it attracted a large number of vehicles. School buses, big rigs, and cars of every description pulled up next to its pumps, waiting and honking for a fill-up, or drivers seeking a quick bathroom stop. When the drivers were told that the station wasn't real, just a set for a new Canadian television show, they drove away disappointed and baffled.

A Minute with the Mayor of Rouleau

WHEN *Corner Gas* began filming in the summer of 2003, no one had the slightest inkling that the series would become such a hit. The folks of Rouleau, too, had no idea the effect the show would have on their town. Once Season 1 hit the air and was watched by over 1 million Canadians, people began to wonder about the real-life Dog River. In the peak of shooting, which runs from May to late September, the set of The Ruby and Corner Gas might see three hundred fans a day. Buses carrying fans who have signed up for a *Corner Gas* tour (offered by CNT Tours; see the Resource Guide on page 206) come every Sunday during filming season.

"No doubt about it, *Corner Gas* has had a positive impact on the town," says Ken Hoffman, the mayor of Rouleau. Ken also runs a business that sells insurance, liquor, greeting cards, and even a few Rouleau souvenirs—all in a single small store. It wasn't *Corner Gas* that came up with the unusual one-stop shop. This multi-purpose store existed long before Brent and his pals came to town, but when the writers saw it, they loved it and wrote it into their scripts.

"Some local residents complain that the roads around town are blocked sometimes while scenes are being shot," explains Ken, from his wood-panelled office, decorated with trophies and plaques. "Others don't like having to go to the post office the long way around while there's filming happening on Main Street. But you'll always have a few people here who don't like change."

Local businesses have done well by *Corner Gas*. Early in the set-building process, the production spent $15,000 at the local lumberyard. During filming for Season 1, it rented all of the rooms at the sole hotel in town, painting and upgrading them to be used as dressing rooms. A once vacant building is now The Stoop, a place popular with out-of-town visitors where you can buy ice cream and a sandwich, plus *Corner Gas* merchandise. Residents have reaped rewards from the show's success, too. Many have served as extras. As well, *Corner Gas* donates money to Rouleau School every year, and helps the town with various community initiatives.

Man about town: Mayor Ken Hoff owns the liquor/insurance store that inspired the show's writers to include one just like it in Dog River.

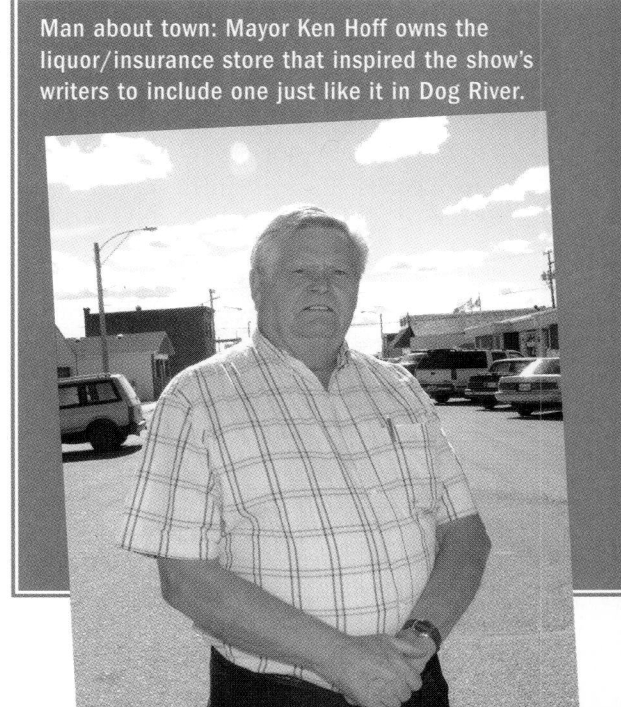

Dog River History 101:
A Rouleau Primer

THE TOWN of Rouleau becomes *Corner Gas* central over the summer. It's a quaint place with a leisurely pace. You could probably have a nap right on Main Street on a Monday morning, if you were so inclined (but don't). Some residents have spent their entire lives here, so it was with more than a bit of curiosity that they greeted the television crew, arriving for the first time in the summer of 2003.

The small farming community was named after Judge Rouleau of Regina. The town sprang from the plains in around 1893. Bargain-basement land prices lured homesteaders from the United States to the area surrounding Rouleau, following the completion of the Canadian Pacific Railway (CPR) line in Saskatchewan from North Portal to Moose Jaw. But the Americans couldn't hack the two or three years of drought facing them, so they packed up their buggies and left town. In the spring of 1900, William Ansley from Watford, Ontario, opened a lumberyard in Rouleau. A boarding house and a barn followed, and boosted the town's population to two hundred. In the fall of 1901, the CPR arrived to survey the town on the north side of the railway tracks. The early pioneers were peeved. They had built their businesses, literally, on the wrong side of the tracks. All the buildings had to be disassembled and moved to the right side of the track. But if you were a carpenter or a lumberyard owner, you probably had a few extra dollars for some pints of ale in those days.

By 1905, Rouleau was in full swing. Generally regarded as one of the neatest, cleanest, and most attractive towns in the West, it was experiencing a bit of a boom. Main Street, now used often for *Corner Gas* scenes, boasted a bowling alley, a Chinese restaurant, the telephone exchange, a barbershop, a bakery, and a gas station called Patron Oil, run by Dad Burns. By 1921, the population of Rouleau swelled to 750. Fast-forward to the 1960s. A cultural boom saw the formation of the Rouleau Community Band and the Roll 'O's Square Dance Club.

For a break from farming life, local residents got involved in sports, and over the years, Rouleau has produced a number of winning teams. In the 1930s, a baseball team known as Frank Keith's Cutworms was acclaimed for its strength at bat. Like any Canadian town, hockey was a favourite. Young kids who didn't have the money for admission to the games would watch them through a knothole in the arena wall. The arena also hosted many a curling bonspiel, from as early as 1904. An abrupt end came to these winter pastimes after a tornado destroyed the building in the summer of 1945. It was rebuilt in 1949. Today, the arena is bustling whenever *Corner Gas* is in town. Off-camera, it serves as an eating area for cast and crew, and it occasionally appears on-camera in episodes.

DOG RIVER
DOG RIVER

Corner Gas Sets in Rouleau

TO VISITING FANS, strolling down Rouleau's Main Street is like popping magically into their televisions screens: So many of the buildings are instantly recognizable.

Outside shots of the Dog River police station are taken in front of a 1906 building that now houses a café called The Stoop. Before cameras roll, the exterior is modified with signage that transforms it into the home of law and order and workplace of Officers Quinton and Pelly.

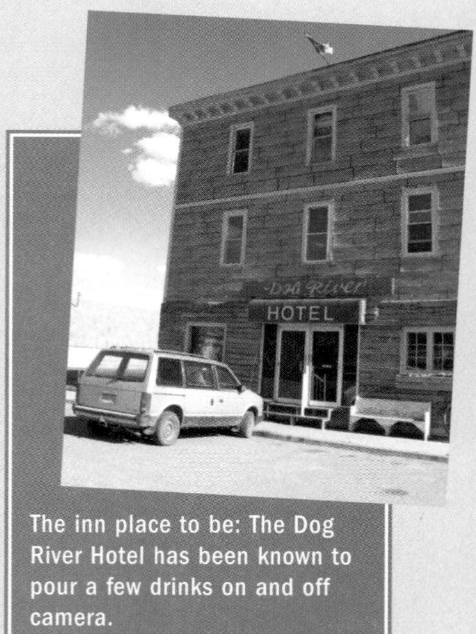

The inn place to be: The Dog River Hotel has been known to pour a few drinks on and off camera.

Justice for all: Karen and Davis stand in front of the Dog River cop shop. When cameras aren't rolling, it's a store and café called The Stoop.

Just down the street is the Dog River Hotel, where many a Dog Riverite has played darts, eaten pickled eggs, and tipped back a few brewskis.

At the end of the street is the post office—an authentic one—that can be spotted in the background in some *Corner Gas* scenes.

Across the street is the media hub of Dog River, the home of the *Dog River Howler.* In a display window, you can see the newspapers, with headlines like "Horseshoe Champ Busted in Drug Scandal," created for episodes of *Corner Gas*. In its real, everyday life, it's a private residence.

Hat trick: Rows of caps adorn the walls of the Dog River Hotel.

Headline hunters: Visitors to Rouleau can see past *Howler* editions used on the show.

Post of the town: Rouleau's post office plays a role in some *Corner Gas* episodes.

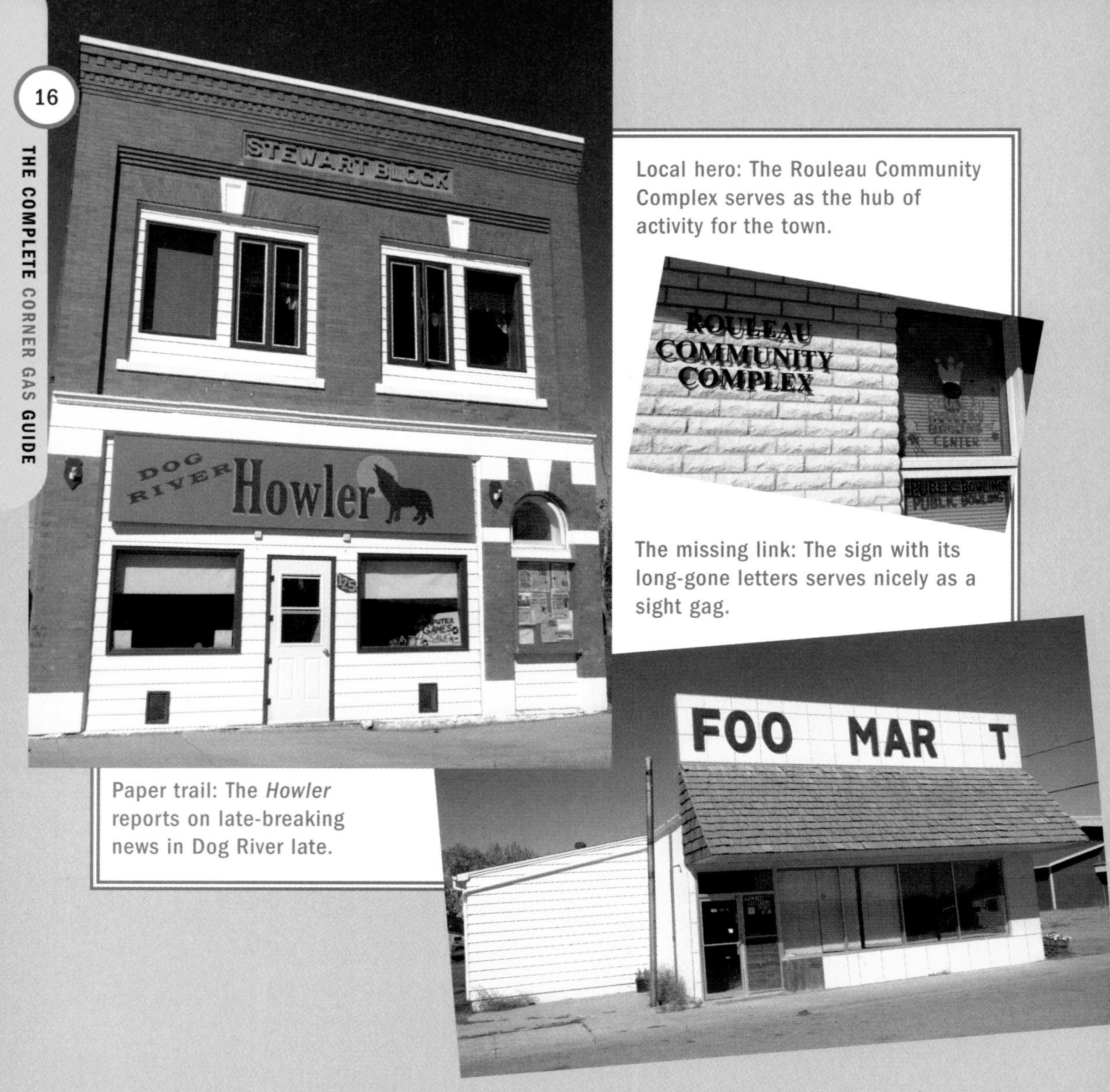

Local hero: The Rouleau Community Complex serves as the hub of activity for the town.

The missing link: The sign with its long-gone letters serves nicely as a sight gag.

Paper trail: The *Howler* reports on late-breaking news in Dog River late.

A hop, skip, and jump from there is the Rouleau Community Complex, which has also been featured in some scenes. Further down is another building often seen on *Corner Gas*. Its sign reads FOO MAR_ _T. Mark Reid, the show's line producer, is often asked whether the name has something to do with the rock band Foo Fighters. It doesn't. The original letters that once adorned the building were found in its basement, but some were missing—there was no *d*, no *k*, no *e*. Mark liked the look of the letters so he had them put back up, despite the gaps in the sign that used to read "Food Market." It made a great visual joke. Now the building is referred to as Foo Mart. When it's not serving as Dog River's grocery store, it is a business that sells orthopaedics to area residents.

The Crew at Work

Get a grip: Gaffer is more like it. Meet Peter Laroque.

A man with vision: Director of photography Ken Krawczyk makes sure everyone is shown in their best light.

The mod squad: Janet Wright gets coiffed and powdered, courtesy of hairstylist Redge Dietrich and makeup artist Krista Stevenson.

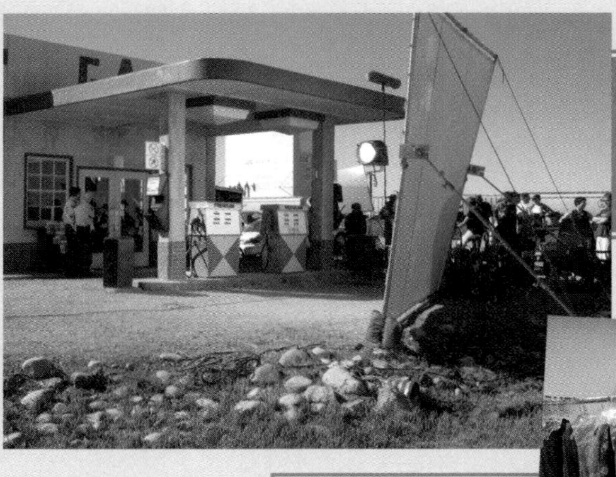

Bright lights, small city: The crew sets up for the next shot in Rouleau.

Designing woman: Brenda Shenher puts together the wardrobe of each character.

Storey time: Fred Ewaniuck and Brent Butt study the script while director David Storey coaches from the sidelines.

Getting a leg up: Line producer Mark Reid puts his best feet forward while trying to balance the budgets for *Corner Gas*.

Soup's on: Chef Marvin Scansen and sous-chef Kevin Dubé take a break after dishing out lunch for the Rouleau cast and crew.

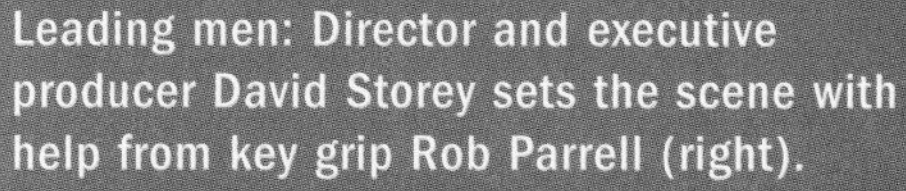

Leading men: Director and executive producer David Storey sets the scene with help from key grip Rob Parrell (right).

Big gang theory: Putting each show together takes the hard work of many in front of and behind the camera. At work here inside the Corner Gas store are Todd Irving (first assistant camera), Alfie Kiernan (first assistant director), April Hall (camera trainee, Season 3), actor Mike O'Brien (as Wes Humboldt), Amanda Park (stand-in), Ryan Mcleod (stand-in), actor Janet Wright, and Dean Schatz (grip).

Playing Favourites

Asking the folks involved in the day-to-day production of *Corner Gas* for their all-time favourite episodes, scenes, and lines from the show caused some alarm. "It's like you want me to choose which one of my children I like best," said one. It's not that bad. When squeezed, everyone confessed a particular fondness for one episode or another. Here's what they had to say.

SARA LONGFELLOW, SET DECORATOR

TOP JOB: To find great stuff to assemble sets that help create the mood.

FAVOURITE EPISODES: Oh Baby (Season 1)—"I love the horror-film feel of the babysitting scenes"; Merry Gasmas (Season 3)—"It was a lot of fun to source cool Christmas decorations."

FAVOURITE SCENES: "I liked Wedding Card (Season 2) because it has scenes showing Davis's sensitive, feminine side—enthusiastically helping plan Oscar and Emma's wedding, and even sewing."

Deck the halls: The Ruby gets ready for Christmas.

Star treks: Kevin McDonald came to Rouleau to appear as tax man Marvin Drey.

BRENT HAYNES, DIRECTOR OF PROGRAMMING FOR THE COMEDY NETWORK

TOP JOB: To develop funny TV shows like *Corner Gas* and help get them on air.

FAVOURITE EPISODE: Tax Man (Season 1)—"It was one of the first written and developed. It was solid from beginning to end and featured a terrific performance by guest star Kevin McDonald."

FAVOURITE LINE: "You wish ..."—Hank to a tiny pooch, while he's out searching for the dog he believes is the Littlest Hobo, in The Littlest Yarbo (Season 3)

DAVID STOREY, EXECUTIVE PRODUCER AND DIRECTOR

TOP JOB: To ensure the show stays on track, and to direct the majority of episodes.

FAVOURITE EPISODE: World's Biggest Thing (Season 1)—"It has some really, really funny parts. Overall, I felt it was an episode that seemed to gel together well."

FAVOURITE LINE: "Is my bum getting warm?"—Brent in Road Worthy (Season 3), when he helps Lacey buy a used car

VIRGINIA THOMPSON, EXECUTIVE PRODUCER

TOP JOB: To make sure the team, the show, CTV, and the fans get the best of *Corner Gas*.

FAVOURITE EPISODE: Tax Man (Season 1) —"It represents many firsts—the first script I read, the first guest star for *Corner Gas*, and our first nomination for an International Emmy Award."

FAVOURITE SCENE: The alliteration-packed scene—peace pie, piece of pie, peach pie—with Emma and Lacey, in Dress for Success (Season 3).

FAVOURITE LINE: "Designing an exercise routine after the guy who sentenced Jesus to death wouldn't sit well with me."—Davis in Pilates Twist (Season 1)

Life of pie: Emma and Lacey get their just desserts.

LOUISE CLARK, DIRECTOR,
WESTERN INDEPENDENT PRODUCTION, CTV

TOP JOB: To develop programming in western Canada.

FAVOURITE EPISODES: Pilates Twist (Season 1); Face Off (Season 1); and Fun Run (Season 3)—"I have so many."

FAVOURITE LINE: "I can't run listening to Jann Arden."—Lacey in Fun Run (Season 3), followed by the scene with Jann Arden running beside Lacey and talking up a storm

Pacemaker: Distraction from singer Jann Arden causes Lacey to train in vain.

HUGH SHANKLAND, PRODUCTION DESIGNER

TOP JOB: To create the look for all the sets used in *Corner Gas*.

FAVOURITE EPISODES: World's Biggest Thing (Season 1)—"It made me giggle"; Trees a Crowd (Season 3)—"It was fun to put together the tree house, something a bit different for us."

MARK FARRELL, PRODUCER AND WRITER

TOP JOB: To write funny scripts and to make funny scripts even funnier.

FAVOURITE EPISODES: "I tried to like my own, but I thought Season 1's Cell Phone was elegant. I also really like World's Biggest Thing (Season 1)—just the idea of it was so smart."

FAVOURITE LINES: "Makes you feel good, doesn't it?"—Hank in Merry Gasmas (Season 3), after a family that everyone assumes is poor shuts the door on him, rejecting the town's charitable handouts that he and his friends were offering

"Bring back some that are square this time, really square. Not those rectangle kind!"—Oscar instructing Emma to get Rice Krispies Squares from the town bake sale, in Comedy Night (Season 1)

CRAIG NORTHEY, WRITER AND PERFORMER OF *CORNER GAS*'S THEME SONGS, "NOT A LOT GOIN' ON" AND "MY HAPPY PLACE"

TOP JOB: To make great music as a musician, singer, and songwriter.

FAVOURITE EPISODES: Comedy Night (Season 1)—"Good laughs"; Security Cam (Season 2)—"I loved Davis zapping himself with the TASER® gun"; and Rock On! (Season 2)—"The Tragically Hip and Colin James are all friends of mine."

MARK REID, LINE PRODUCER

TOP JOB: To monitor shows to ensure they stay on budget and finish on time.

FAVOURITE EPISODE: Pilates Twist (Season 1)—"It was so clever and so funny."

FAVOURITE WORD CREATIONS: "I like some of the words that the writers make up, like *style-omfort* and *dingledork*."

ANDREW CARR, STORY EDITOR

TOP JOB: To come up with funny storylines for episodes.

FAVOURITE EPISODES: Key to the Future (Season 3)—"I love the idea of Hank being psychic, based on his vague dreams."

"Of my own scripts, I like Face Off (Season 1), because it got the cast together in a different environment."

Leader of the pack: Coach Burrows rallies her team.

KEVIN WHITE, EXECUTIVE STORY EDITOR

TOP JOB: To write funny scripts and to boost their funny quotient.

FAVOURITE EPISODES: Lost and Found (Season 2); Fun Run (Season 3); and Block Party (Season 3)—"There are bits in all of them that are fun."

FAVOURITE SCENE:

Hank: "I don't know about this sweet potato pie. The potatoes aren't sweet."

Karen: "Did you buy sweet potatoes?"

Hank: "It's kind of hard to tell until you get them home and taste them."

—from Mail Fraud (Season 3)

PAUL MATHER, SUPERVISING PRODUCER/WRITER

TOP JOB: To make sure all roads head straight for funny.

FAVOURITE EPISODES: Ruby Reborn (Season 1); Hook, Line and Sinker (Season 1).

FAVOURITE LINE: "Sorry, kids. No Christmas this year."—Wade the garbage man, after losing his job because Oscar is picking up all the street trash himself, in Lost and Found (Season 2)

BRENDA SHENHER, COSTUME DESIGNER

TOP JOB: To dress the actors and to shop for the actors' wardrobes.

FAVOURITE EPISODES: Hurry Hard (Season 2)—"Like Brent, I too grew up curling in those small-town rinks where they had shelves for your glass of rye 'n' 7 and ashtrays built in along the sides of the sheets of ice." Also high on her list: "I laugh at almost anything Oscar says and does, like sending an email to an unknown couple in China in Mail Fraud (Season 3). That is something I can relate to!"

FAVOURITE LINES: "I love all of Davis's lines, like '*I'm* pretty.'"—Davis to Karen, in Grad '68 (Season 1)

SCOTT HENDERSON, SENIOR DIRECTOR OF PROGRAMMING COMMUNICATIONS, CTV

TOP JOB: To boost the profile of network shows like *Corner Gas* by working with media across the country.

FAVOURITE EPISODE: Merry Gasmas (Season 3)—"I liked it not only because the episode reached an audience of nearly 3 million—the most ever for a *Corner Gas* episode—but because it's uniquely Canadian, totally charming, and as funny as Christmas pudding."

FAVOURITE LINES:

Lacey: "You made the call?"

Airport official: "Well, no. The airline made the call. I don't make calls. I mean, I can make a call, like if they want me to call somebody. But no, this kind of call is their call. They make the call. And then they call me."

—from a scene where Lacey is trying to get to Toronto for Christmas, in Merry Gasmas (Season 3)

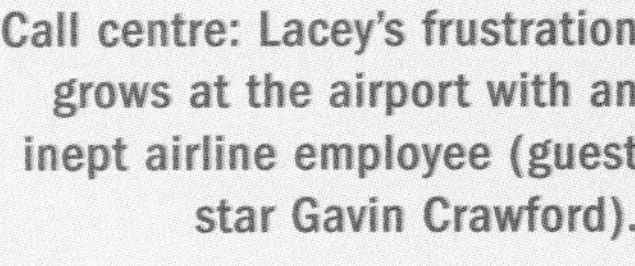

Call centre: Lacey's frustration grows at the airport with an inept airline employee (guest star Gavin Crawford).

SARAH FEDORCHUK, ASSOCIATE PRODUCER/NEW PROJECT DEVELOPMENT, VÉRITÉ FILMS

TOP JOB: To serve as a liaison between the producers and everyone else involved in the show, and to assist the author writing this official guide to *Corner Gas*.

FAVOURITE EPISODE: Security Cam (Season 2)—"The scene where Davis is 'auditioning' for Brent in The Ruby, for what Davis calls security cam plays, kills me every time. I'm giggling right now just thinking about it. I also love the scene where Davis shocks himself with his new TASER gun as he is acting out his scene in front of the security camera."

FAVOURITE LINE: "My name is Davis Quinton. I'm auditioning for one of Lacey's security plays. For this scene, I'll be using a TASER gun ..."—Davis to the security camera, in Security Cam (Season 2)

ED ROBINSON, SENIOR VICE-PRESIDENT, COMEDY AND VARIETY PROGRAMMING, CTV

TOP JOB: To develop and to discover the best comedy and variety shows for the network's schedule.

FAVOURITE EPISODES: "I like Hook, Line and Sinker (Season 1). Everyone is trying to make Oscar think that he is losing his mind. Also right up there are Slow Pitch, Hurry Hard, Rock On! (all Season 2), and Merry Gasmas (Season 3).

FAVOURITE LINE: "Jackass!"—usually said by Oscar but by other characters too throughout the show

SUSANNE BOYCE, PRESIDENT, CTV PROGRAMMING AND CHAIR OF THE CTV MEDIA GROUP

TOP JOB: To put together a successful program lineup by buying and developing great shows.

FAVOURITE EPISODE: Ruby Reborn (Season 1)—"It will always be my favourite because of all the feelings associated with it as the very first episode of *Corner Gas*."

FAVOURITE SCENE: "Every time I think of the bit where Pamela Wallin steals a chocolate bar from the Corner Gas store in Hook, Line and Sinker (Season 1), I crack up."

FAVOURITE LINE: "*The Life of Pi*? That's my favourite maritime tiger book."—Wanda in Comedy Night (Season 1)

MIKE COSENTINO, VICE-PRESIDENT, COMMUNICATIONS CTV INC.

TOP JOB: To oversee communications, press, and publicity for CTV Inc. (consisting of CTV Network plus specialty and digital services).

FAVOURITE EPISODE: Tax Man (Season 1)—"Kevin McDonald guest stars, giving a memorable performance as Marvin Drey, a Canada Customs and Revenue agent. Drey turns the town upside down with his innocent questions for Oscar. The ripple effect has The Ruby charging for coffee, creating a divide in the police force, which starts issuing revenge parking tickets. Brent Leroy describes the scene to CTV Newsnet anchor Dan Matheson, the first of many fantasy sequences to come in the series. Tax Man was also affirmation that we had a bona fide hit on our hands—the real thing."

FAVOURITE SCENE: "In Tax Man (Season 1), when Officer Karen Pelly volunteers to pay for coffee, thereby breaking a long-standing tradition and provoking her sidekick Davis Quinton to liken her to infamous honest cop Serpico. Davis warns that she is at risk of being shunned by the whole force, which has become accustomed to freebies. Karen reminds him: 'We are the whole force.'"

FAVOURITE LINE: "One of the local cops went kind of nuts with the parking tickets and then my old man vowed pretty kind of a revenge thing and that went back and forth for a while, the whole town started some kind of a feud thing and long story short, I'm the only one left alive."—Brent Leroy deadpans to Dan Matheson in an interview for CTV Newsnet, in Tax Man (Season 1)

The Look

Dressed for Success

EACH CHARACTER has his or her own unique fashion sense … or a proud lack thereof. There's plenty of method behind the madness when it comes to what's being worn by anyone who appears on-camera. Gemini Award–nominated costume designer Brenda Shenher learned to sew as a kid through the 4-H Club in Viceroy, Saskatchewan, but her best instruction came from a master teacher—her mom. Brenda dresses the cast (not literally, they can all do that nicely by themselves) and spends plenty of time shopping for costumes. A peak into her notebook reveals the style and the substance behind the seams at *Corner Gas*.

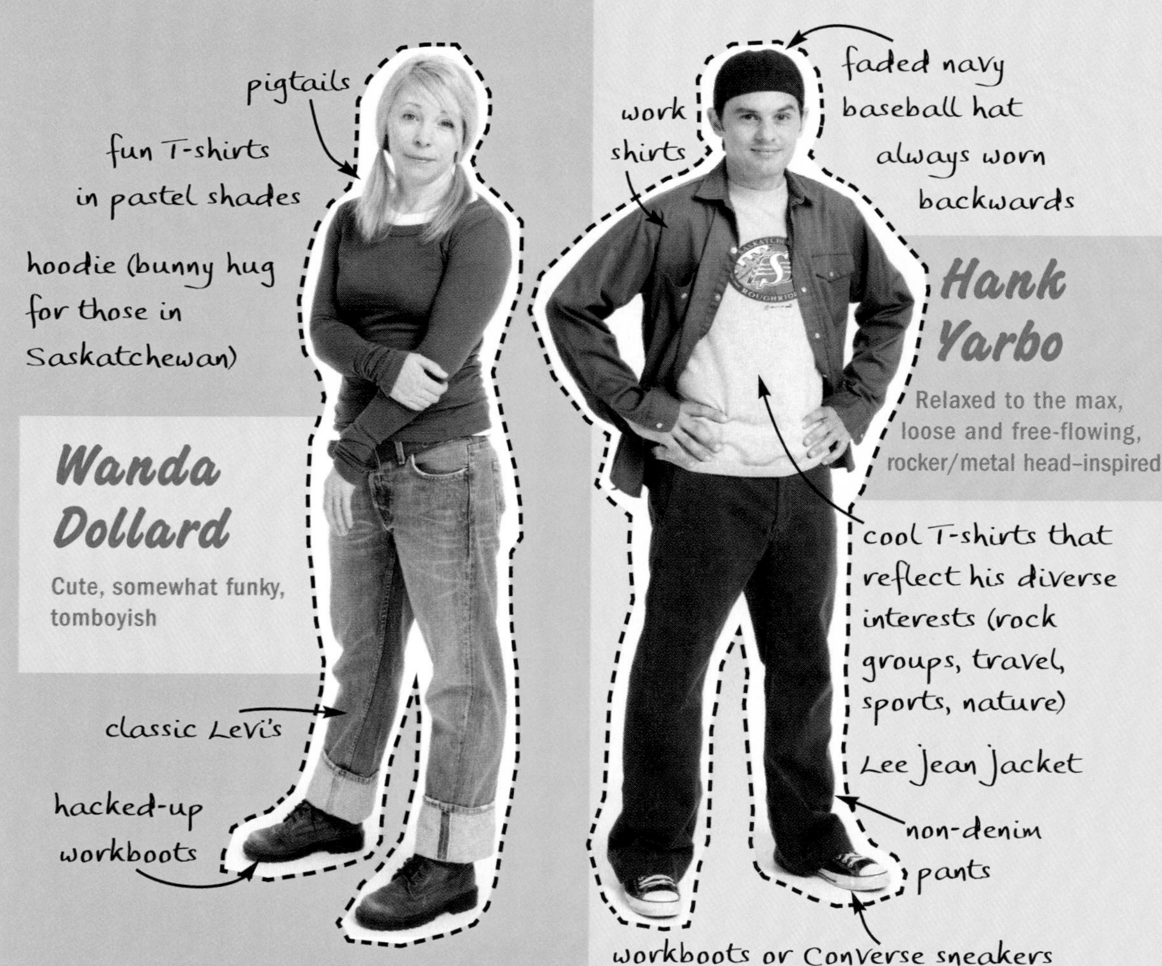

Wanda Dollard

Cute, somewhat funky, tomboyish

Hank Yarbo

Relaxed to the max, loose and free-flowing, rocker/metal head–inspired

Oscar Leroy

Part farmer, part rancher, part blue-collar working man, mixed with a down-home folksy feel

straw Bing Crosby-style hat for special occasions

green farmer hat with white embroidered oil derrick

work shirts with glasses case and pen in the pocket

cardigan

dress-up shirts (with retro patterns like seahorses and sailboats)

western-style belt buckle

stretchy polyester Wranglers

runners with Velcro straps

Emma Leroy

Homespun sophistication that's classic yet oh so casual

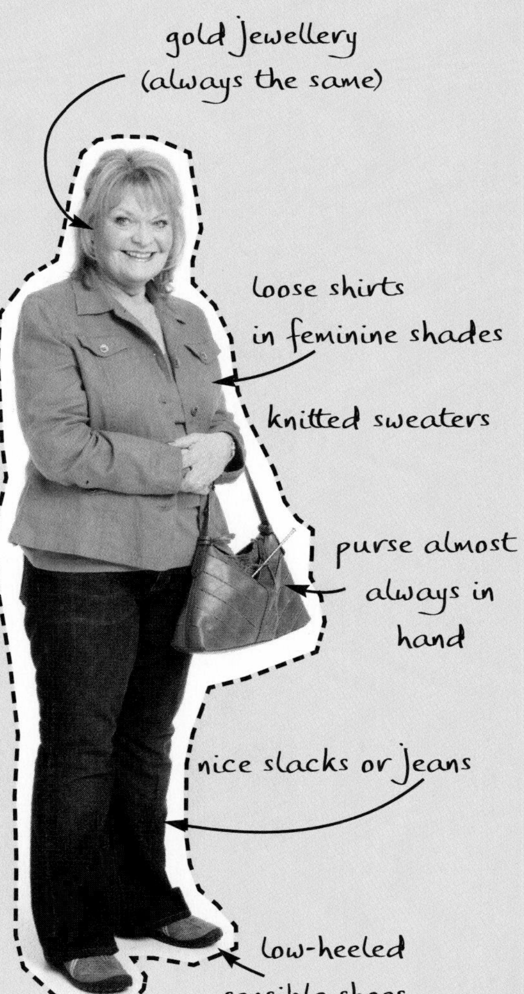

Brent Leroy

Never pretentious, never fancy, and comfort is king

Lacey Burrows

Soft and sweet, combining the elegance of Audrey Hepburn with the sexiness of Elizabeth Taylor circa 1960

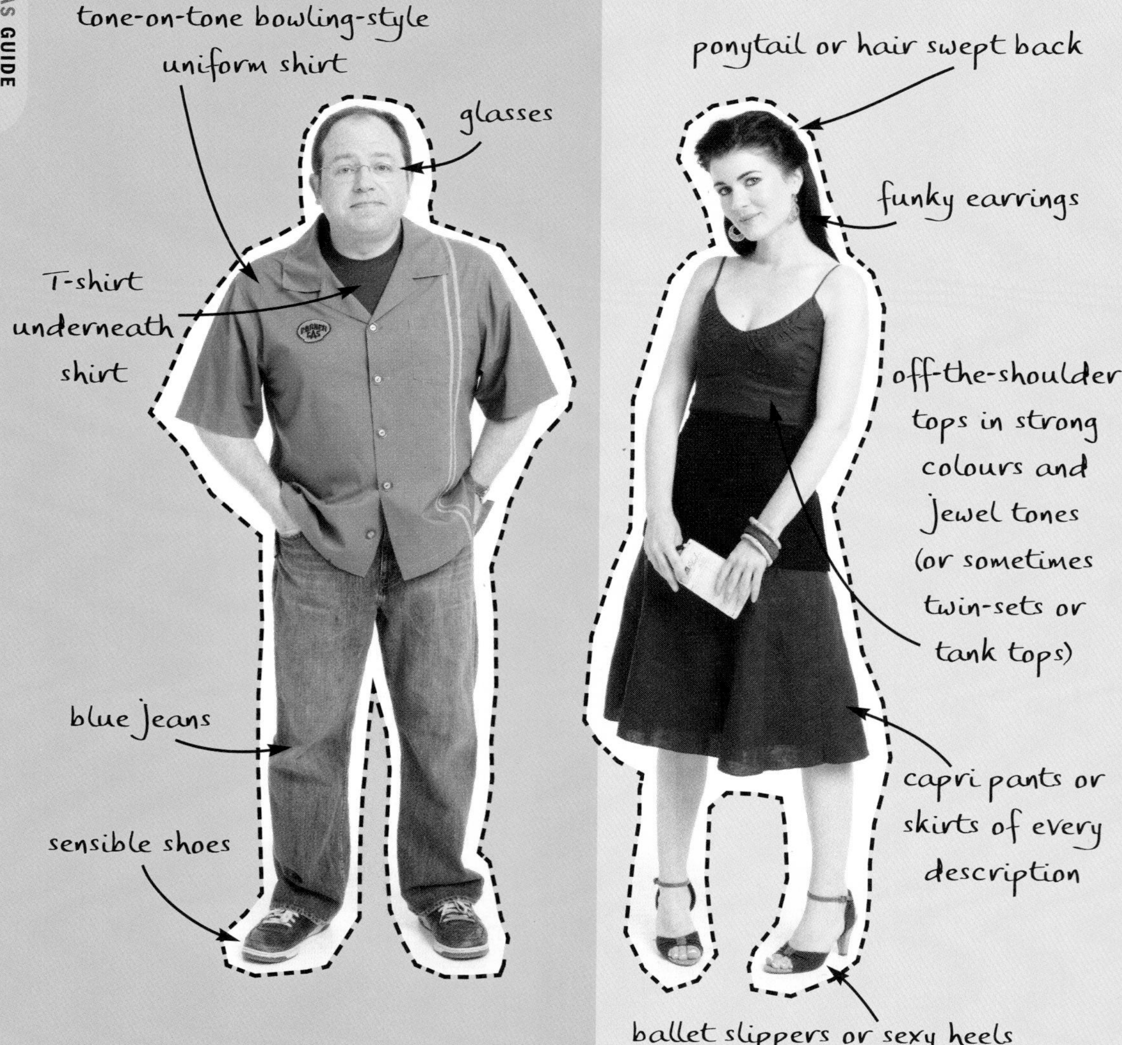

Davis Quinton

By day, buttoned-down police officer; by night, a sexy vibe with a touch of at-home-on-the-range cowboy chic

Karen Pelly

By day, buttoned-down police officer; by night, sporty yet spicy

For Karen and Davis, you might notice that they do not look exactly like the actual RCMP officers who work in certain areas of Saskatchewan. Midway through Season 1, you may have noticed that even the red stripes down the side of their trousers disappeared. Strange? The work of alien forces? No. The show initially contacted the Mounted Police Foundation (which owns the rights to portrayals of the force) to arrange permission for Davis and Karen to appear as RCMP officers, but it was unable to reach an agreement. Since Karen and Davis could not be depicted as RCMP officers, details of their uniforms were changed so that it would be clear to viewers that they weren't supposed to be members of the RCMP.

Setting the Scene

WHEN YOU'RE STARTING a television series from scratch, every detail needs to be gone over countless times. What should The Ruby look like? What kind of furniture would a couple like Oscar and Emma have? What kind of sheets would Hank sleep on? What kind of knick-knacks would Davis have on his desk at police headquarters?

To figure out all these details, *Corner Gas* has production designer Hugh Shankland. His job is to come up with what the set should look like, based on the needs of the production (things like movable walls are a nifty feature) and the personality of the characters who inhabit a house or a business. "There's almost a subliminal effect that is created," says Hugh. "Everything from the colour of the curtains to the art on the wall has psychological nuances."

Once Hugh determines the mood of a room, with input from the show's director and from Ken Krawczyk, the director of photography, it's up to set decorator Sara Longfellow and her department to make it

It's all mine: Production designer Hugh Shankland shows off the finished *Corner Gas* set.

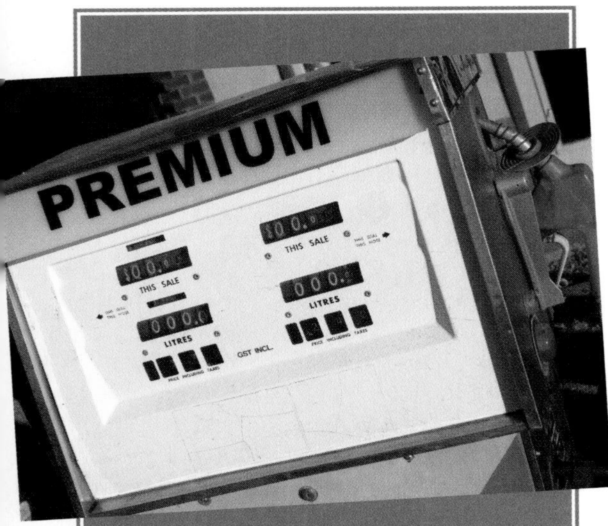

Petrol Canada: Vintage pump purchased in Saskatchewan from a former gas station owner.

happen. They search high and low for the perfect items to turn a set into a place that fits the scene and the characters. One challenge of shooting in Saskatchewan is that there isn't a movie prop house in the province, so the hunt for items needed for the show can lead to some hardcore investigation, on par with that of a CSI team.

Even after three seasons, the residents of Dog River still have an air of mystery to them. For a glimpse into the far recesses of their minds, let's take a look at the places where they work, live, and hang out for a few clues on what makes them tick.

Corner Gas

THE GAS STATION has been a part of Dog River for a long while. Oscar's dad might even have owned it before Oscar, then Brent, took it over. It has a vintage feel, but you can tell that it's been well looked after and modernized here and there over the years. Oscar might be cranky, but he's always proud to have been the proprietor of the gas station. Brent, a poster boy for neatness, likes everything just so. The details:

THE GAS PUMPS. It took days of hunting to find ones from the 1970s. Sara eventually located the former owner of a gas station who had an old set of pumps in his shed and was willing to sell them for $250 for the pair. After a fresh paint job and a bit of retooling, the pumps were camera-ready.

NO-SMOKING SIGN, bought from a junkyard.

OLD WINDOWS in the store. Hugh wanted old glass to add a bit of texture and depth to the windows. It was a real pain, but he discovered what he needed at a used lumber yard.

Faux fruit: Made of 100 percent all-natural plastic.

SNACK FOODS from Canadian companies, including Old Dutch potato chips and Hawkin's Cheezies (Brent's favourite). Hawkin's sent so many bags of Cheezies that they fed the cast and crew for an entire season. If you look closely, you can still see orange stains on their fingers.

SNACK RACK from Nutty Club, a Winnipeg-based company.

MILK CARTONS—real containers, but empty, since the coolers don't actually work.

MAPS AND POSTCARDS, horoscopes, and a cowboy head on the shelf behind the counter.

PLASTIC FRUIT

MAGAZINES: over the seasons, some have been real and others, like *Bean Soup*, are creations for the show.

PLASTIC SODA CARRIERS

Licensed to thrill: Vehicle plates from Saskatchewan adorn the door of Corner Gas.

Strange but true: In Season 1, the set decorators were not allowed to use real chocolate bars. Before you can use a real product on a television show, you need to get permission from the company. That first year, before the show had even aired and it was still an unknown entity, there were a lot of *no thank-yous*. So, candy bars had to be created from scratch. Styrofoam forms were wrapped in foil and then with labels designed by Dan Wright in the art department. If you look closely, they have made-up names—Hughmongous (a nod to the production designer Hugh Shankland), Sweet Sara (named for Sara Longfellow, set decorator), Morgan's Milk, Danny Bar, and

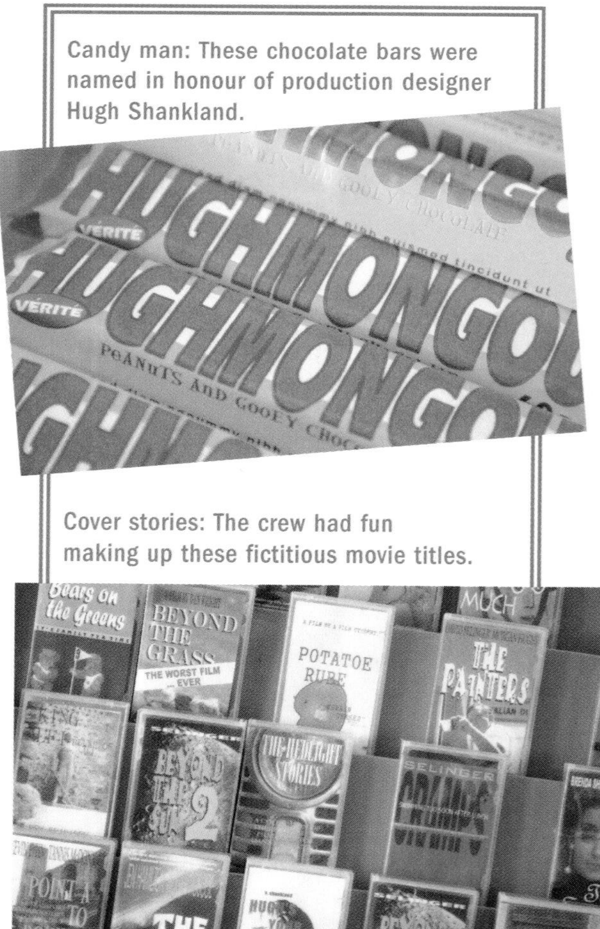

Candy man: These chocolate bars were named in honour of production designer Hugh Shankland.

Cover stories: The crew had fun making up these fictitious movie titles.

Jennirous—inside jokes by the crew. Now that the show has become a huge success, many companies are vying to put their products on the shelves of Corner Gas.

The crew also had fun with the video rack, making up the fictitious titles and using crew members' names to create videotapes you'll never see at Blockbuster. Check out some of the titles: *Safari Ken* (in honour of director of photography Ken Krawczyk), *The Boy Who Saw Too Much, Go Climb a Tree, Bears on the Greens, The Red Jacket, Beyond the Grass, Potatoe Rube, School Bus—The Scariest Ride You'll Ever Take, King Alfi: Ruler of All* (a reference to first assistant director Alfie Keirnan), and *The Royal Goose.*

Well accessorized: The set dec department researched vintage diners to make sure it found the right props.

The Ruby

LACEY BURROWS, the new owner of Dog River's favourite, maybe only, diner is a sophisticated, big-city woman. The diner's decor matches her personality. It has feminine touches—pretty curtains, flowers in vases on the tables, and interesting art on the walls. Contrary to what Hank thought in Season 1's Ruby Reborn, Lacey didn't turn the diner into a gay bar. Indeed, it looks as though Lacey's Aunt Ruby, the original owner, may have opened

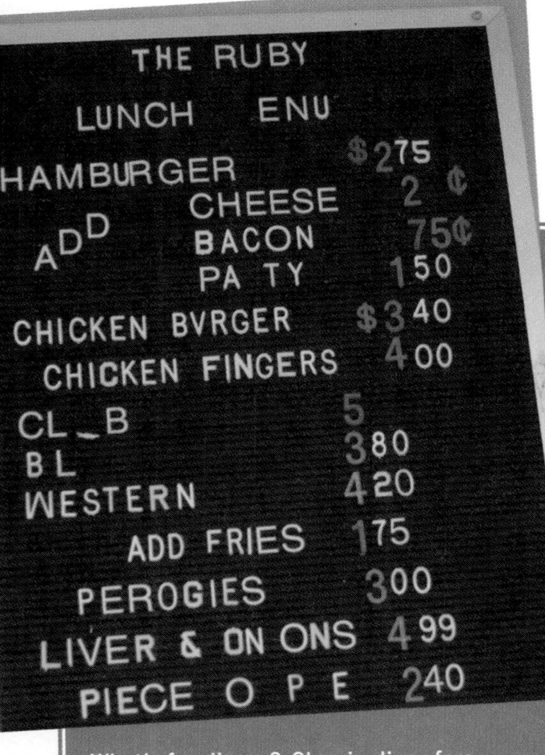

What's for dinner? Classic diner fare never goes out of style.

Meal ticket: Even The Ruby menu looks real.

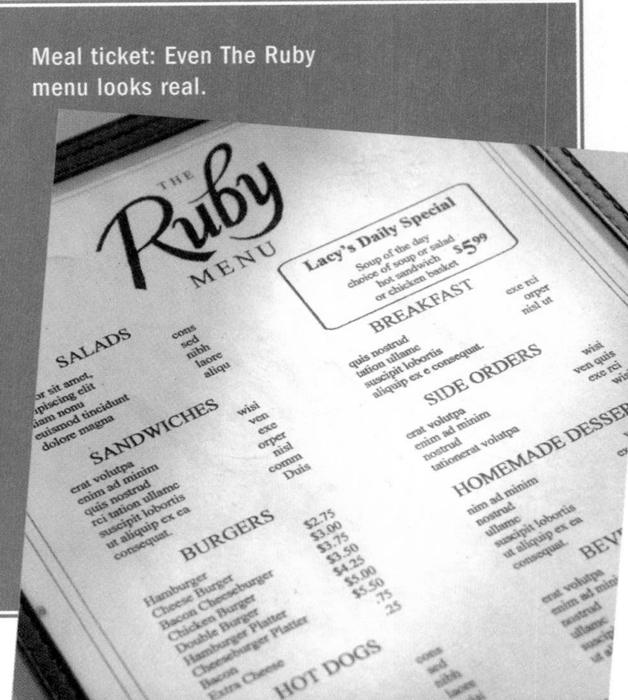

The Ruby in the 1950s, judging by its stainless steel furnishings and old-fashioned red booths. The details:

1950S FRIDGE and coffee grinder.

ANTIQUE CASH REGISTER, bought second-hand in Regina. It weighed so much (more than 45 kilograms) that the diner's counter had to be reinforced to prevent it from collapsing under the weight.

YUMMY CAKES and baked goods, made of Styrofoam by a company in Toronto. In Season 1, the crew complained after real loaves of bread became mouldy and stinky with age.

FRIDGE MAGNETS, including one that plays music.

A PAINTING on the wall titled *Clouds by Craven*, by Saskatchewan artist and former *Corner Gas* set decorator Sara McCudden.

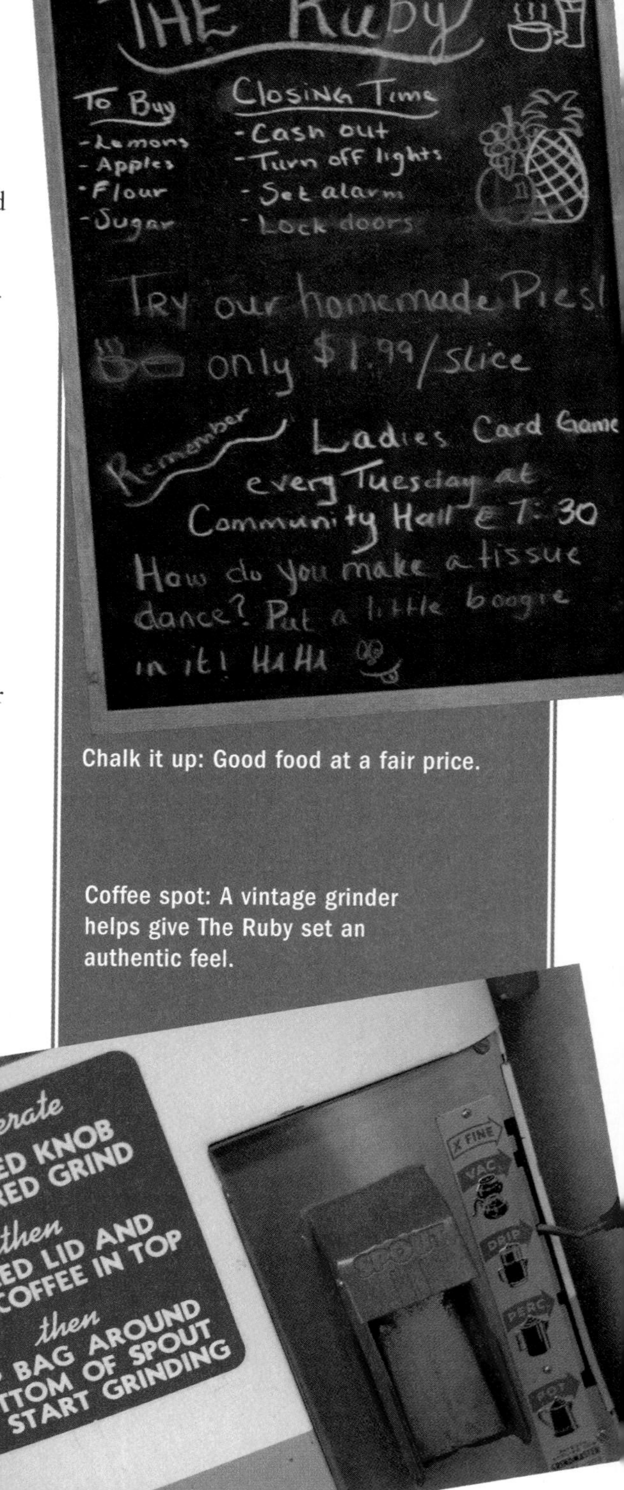

THE Ruby
To Buy
-Lemons
-Apples
-Flour
-Sugar
Closing Time
-Cash out
-Turn off lights
-Set alarm
-Lock doors
Try our homemade Pies!
only $1.99/slice
Remember
Ladies Card Game
every Tuesday at
Community Hall @ 7:30
How do you make a tissue
dance? Put a little boogie
in it! HaHa
To Operate
MOVE RED KNOB
TO DESIRED GRIND
then
LIFT RED LID AND
POUR COFFEE IN TOP
then
SLIP BAG AROUND
BOTTOM OF SPOUT
TO START GRINDING
X FINE
VAC
DRIP
PERC
POT

Chalk it up: Good food at a fair price.

Coffee spot: A vintage grinder helps give The Ruby set an authentic feel.

Rough and ready: A bobble-head from the Saskatchewan Roughriders sits by The Ruby's cash register.

Cash and carry: This old beast weighs more than 45 kilograms.

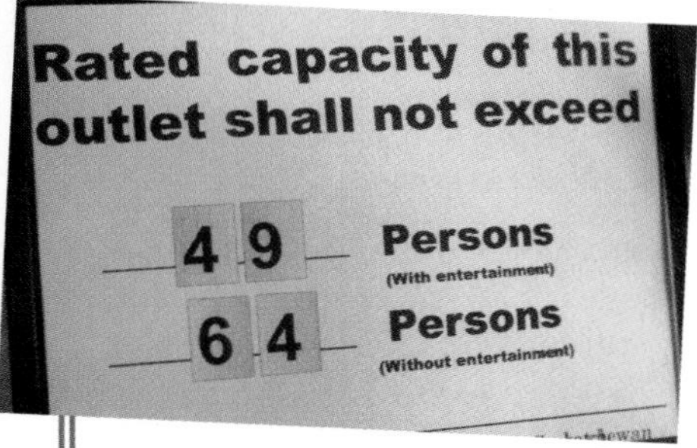

Rated capacity of this outlet shall not exceed
49 Persons
(With entertainment)
64 Persons
(Without entertainment)

Crowd control: Just how many Dog Riverites can you fit into The Ruby?

Oscar and Emma's House

OSCAR AND EMMA have probably lived here all of their lives. The house is decorated with objects they've accumulated over many years. They've never done a huge renovation—God knows, Oscar would be too busy cussing at butterflies to get anything done. You won't find anything overly cutesy here—Emma wouldn't stand for it. She's a practical, no-fuss kind of woman. The details:

EMMA'S COLLECTIONS (spoons, salt-and-pepper shakers, plates).

COMFY OLD COUCH with a 1970s-era afghan or quilt.

VINTAGE STEREO

LISTS OF THINGS for Oscar to do, on the fridge.

Home sweet home: Oscar and Emma's place is more cozy than kitschy.

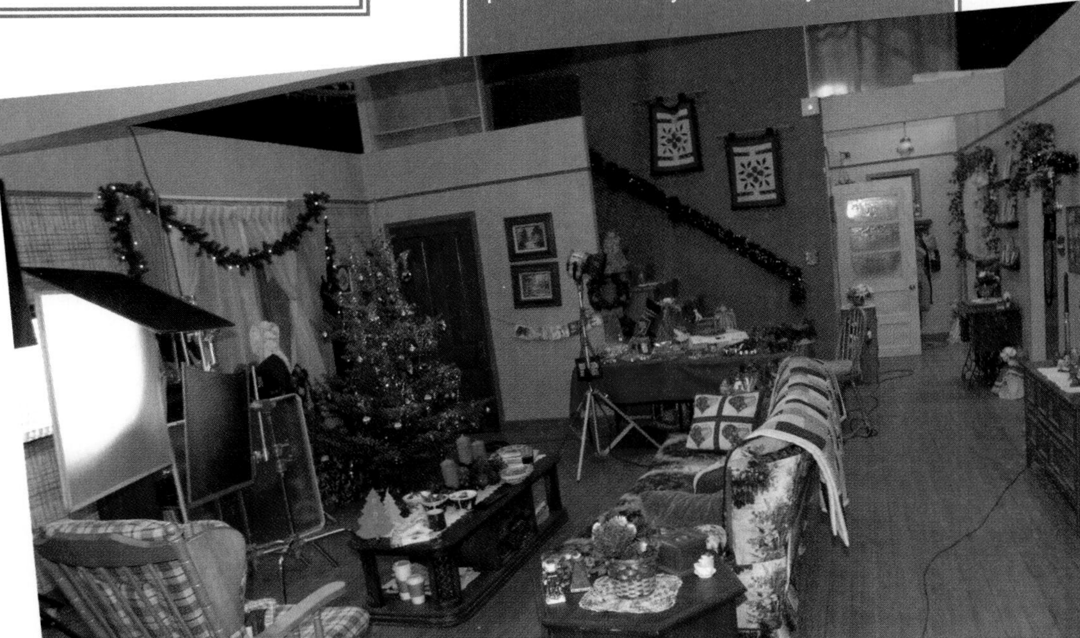

A fridge too far: Emma decorates it with various doodads.

Freeze frame: Oscar and Emma's history together in photos.

Brent's House

VIEWERS HAVEN'T VISITED Brent's bachelor pad very often—most of his life is spent at the gas station or at The Ruby swilling coffee. When they did, what they saw was a neat and tidy living room with everything in its place, and a bedroom with furniture that looked as though it came from his parents' home. Brent is a minimalist and every bit the perennial bachelor. The details:

BIG-SCREEN TELEVISION

GUITAR (something Brent Butt can play quite well in real life).

Wanda's Home

IN SEASON 1, we saw Brent and Lacey attempting to control Wanda's demonic six-year-old son, Tanner, in the Oh Baby episode. To add to the terror of babysitting such a child, the house (located on a farm outside Rouleau) was dark, creepy, and had lots of hiding places. Wanda is much too busy reading and expanding her mind to worry about something as mundane as housework—hence its messy state. The details:

OODLES OF TOYS scattered everywhere.

TEXTBOOKS

EXOTIC ARTS AND CRAFTS, like batik, to show her worldly side.

PILES OF PAPERS

Hank's Abode

SOME MEN never quite grow up. Hank is a poster child for arrested development. He still lives like a student, though he's not. He has a lot of varied interests, including astronomy, something we discovered with the visit to his bedroom in the Block Party episode (Season 3). You get the feeling that if Hank had to disassemble a car engine, he'd do it on his living-room floor. Chaos is the order of the day. The details:

OLD FLORAL COUCH

FISHING TACKLE

STUFFED FISH mounted on a wood plaque.

GUN in a wall rack.

SPORTS PARAPHERNALIA from the Saskatchewan Roughriders, and from the Regina Pats of the Western Hockey League.

PILLOWCASE with planet, stars, and moon pattern (purchased from a Salvation Army thrift store by the set dec department).

Desk set: Davis has eclectic tastes, from rhinos to rocks.

The Police Station

THERE'S A SENSE of history in this old building. It was renovated at some point to expose the brick walls. It's neat and organized, because both Davis and Karen like a big dose of order with their law. The details:

DAVIS'S DESK: On top are assorted items, including, at one time or another, a model police car, a plastic rhinoceros, and a rock collection.

***COSMOPOLITAN* MAGAZINES** in Davis's desk drawer—required reading for any metrosexual.

FRAMED BRONZE MEDAL behind Davis's desk. It belongs to actor Lorne Cardinal. In 2005, he and his rugby team, the Strathcona Druids, took third place at the World Masters Games, held in Edmonton. Having the medal there is his way of giving a shout-out to his teammates.

KAREN'S DESK holds sticky notes and cosmetics (tubes of lipstick and nail polish).

ROLLER SKATES AND A BOTTLE OF SCOTCH in the cupboard behind Karen's desk.

The simple life: The desk of by-the-book cop Karen lacks extraneous objects.

In Tune with *Corner Gas*

CRAIG NORTHEY had not seen an episode of *Corner Gas* (none was available for him to view), but when long-time friend Brent Butt asked him to come up with a theme song for the show, he forged ahead anyway. Through chatting with Brent, Craig, the founding member of the acclaimed Canadian band Odds, picked up key phrases that would form the basis of the song's lyrics. Brent wanted a song "that you could drive across the Great Plains to." For help, Craig hooked up with Jesse Valenzuela of the Gin Blossoms. The result was "Not A Lot Goin' On." Initially, Brent wasn't sold on the first line, "You can tell me that your dog ran away / then tell me that it took three days," a twist on the classic Prairie joke. But when Brent listened to it again, he realized how well it fit the humour of *Corner Gas*.

Craig submitted a second song for consideration as well. Brent had told him that *Corner Gas* had sequences where he would go to his "happy place." Knowing a good thing when he heard it, Craig spun those words into "My Happy Place" as another option for the opening song. The producers loved that song too, and ended up using both, with "Not A Lot Goin' On" taking the kick-off spot. After Craig got a rough cut of the Tax Man episode, it confirmed his gut feeling that he had accurately captured the show's easygoing spirit with his words and music.

When Brent and company toured across the country for *Corner Gas Live,* Craig joined them. "It was great to see fans so excited to hear the full version of the theme song," says Craig. "Now, it's become a kind of Prairie anthem. I'm just happy that I could be a part of the success of *Corner Gas*."

"My Happy Place"

I don't know the same things
you don't know
I don't know
I just don't know

Ooooh, it's a great big place
Full of nothing but space
And it's my happy place

I don't know
Yes, you do ... ungh
You just won't admit it
I don't know

"Not A Lot Goin' On"

You can tell me that your dog ran away
Then tell me that it took three days
I've heard every joke
I've heard every word you say

CHORUS:
You think there's not a lot goin' on
Look closer baby, you're so wrong
And that's why you can stay so long
Where there's not a lot goin' on

I roll my eyes back into my happy place
I'm always going to need this
sense of space
In the amber waves under a rolling cloud
I can't hear what you say 'cause you're
talking so loud
How many times you gonna
get me wrong?
Yeah yeah yeah

REPEAT CHORUS

You could use a glass half full
of something strong
To help you see the emperor with
nothing on
Double your dose if it's over the counter
'cause you're sad
Yeah yeah yeah yeah yeah yeah
out of towner

With the rain, you could get
lightning on you
Strikes twice, you better believe it
Under a sky that's always wrapped
around you
Good luck, you know you'll never need it

REPEAT CHORUS

Note worthy: Craig Northey and Doug Elliott croon in tune during *Corner Gas Live!*

Doing It Write

A TYPICAL STORY MEETING with the writers in attendance might start with the words "What if ...?" or "It would be funny if ..." From there, the tall tales are spun. "What if Hank loses his driver's licence? What if Emma takes up poker? What if ...?" Possible storylines spill from the writers, and sometimes the ideas can get pretty loopy, though each and every one is a potential winner.

"We throw all of our ideas out there," explains Brent, "even the bad ones. Even a bad idea can lead to a good one. You get crazy ideas, then work from there backwards to the point where they might work into a nice little story."

Typically at the beginning of production for a new season, usually sometime in the spring, the writers gather to share their ideas. Each writer brings a unique twist on humour. Kevin White gathers inspiration from real-life events that happened to him or to a friend or to a friend of a friend. In the Season 3 episode Mail Fraud, for example, he vented his frustration with people who sign up to bring the napkins or plastic utensils to potlucks. In that episode, Karen was the one who made sure that Davis wasn't going to get away with just napkin duty. As Kevin says, "Dumb is funny."

Paul Mather, the supervising producer—or "showrunner," as the position is called in show-biz circles—also works reality into his scripts. He once sublet his Vancouver apartment to a guy who didn't have a sense of smell. Paul didn't think much of it—until the tenant burnt a hole in his rug after a lamp dropped onto it and the rug began to smoulder.

For other writers, like Mark Farrell, their obsessions seep into storylines. Both Mark and Brent are comic book freaks. You'll hear frequent references to them and often see Brent reading a comic book in a scene. In Season 1's World's Biggest Thing, Brent mentions Peter Parker, a name that comic fans know as the everyday name of Spider-Man. Mark is also a sci-fi fan. Any time you hear a reference to *Battlestar Galactica, Star Wars* (like in Season's 1 Hook, Line and Sinker episode), or *Star Trek,* you can bet Mark Farrell was the one at the keyboard. Mark's other secret passion is *Buffy the Vampire Slayer,* so be all ears for nods to his favourite killer of blood-sucking beasts.

With Paul Mather, it's clothing gone awry that tickles his funny bone. He has penned three clothes-related episodes. One focuses on shirts (in Season 1's Pilates Twist, Hank's and Brent's fashion worlds collide when they wear the same plaid ones); another on shoes (Davis gets new ones in Season 2's Pandora's Wine); and yet another was all about pants (Oscar finds a perfectly good pair on the side of the road in Season 2's Lost and Found).

"That's my clothing trilogy," says Paul. "I doubt I'll be writing more. We have a list of top five *Corner Gas* script clichés and the clothing storylines might have to go on it."

The writers might sound somewhat nutty, but they're some of the very best in the business. If you ask the cast why *Corner Gas* has become such a success, unanimously they say the strength of the show's writing plays a big, big part. That's not too surprising, since many of the writers have penned their own material as stand-up comics. If you think you've got something funny to say, you'll find out within seconds of delivering a punchline in front of a live audience whether you're right or painfully wrong. The *Corner Gas* writers have proven that they know a lot about funny.

In an episode of *Corner Gas,* typically three storylines are woven together into a single show. Once the writers have a whack of ideas that Brent likes, they go ahead and do a three-page outline. They figure out on paper what the scenes will be and which characters are in them, and then structure the scenes so that they can be worked into an episode. All the story editors and a handful of CTV execs weigh in on the outlines, sending back notes. The original concept gets tweaked; some notes are incorporated, others tossed; and then the outline is ready to be turned into a draft script that will include dialogue for

Air of mystery: When there is truly nothin' goin' on, Brent amuses himself with strange pastimes.

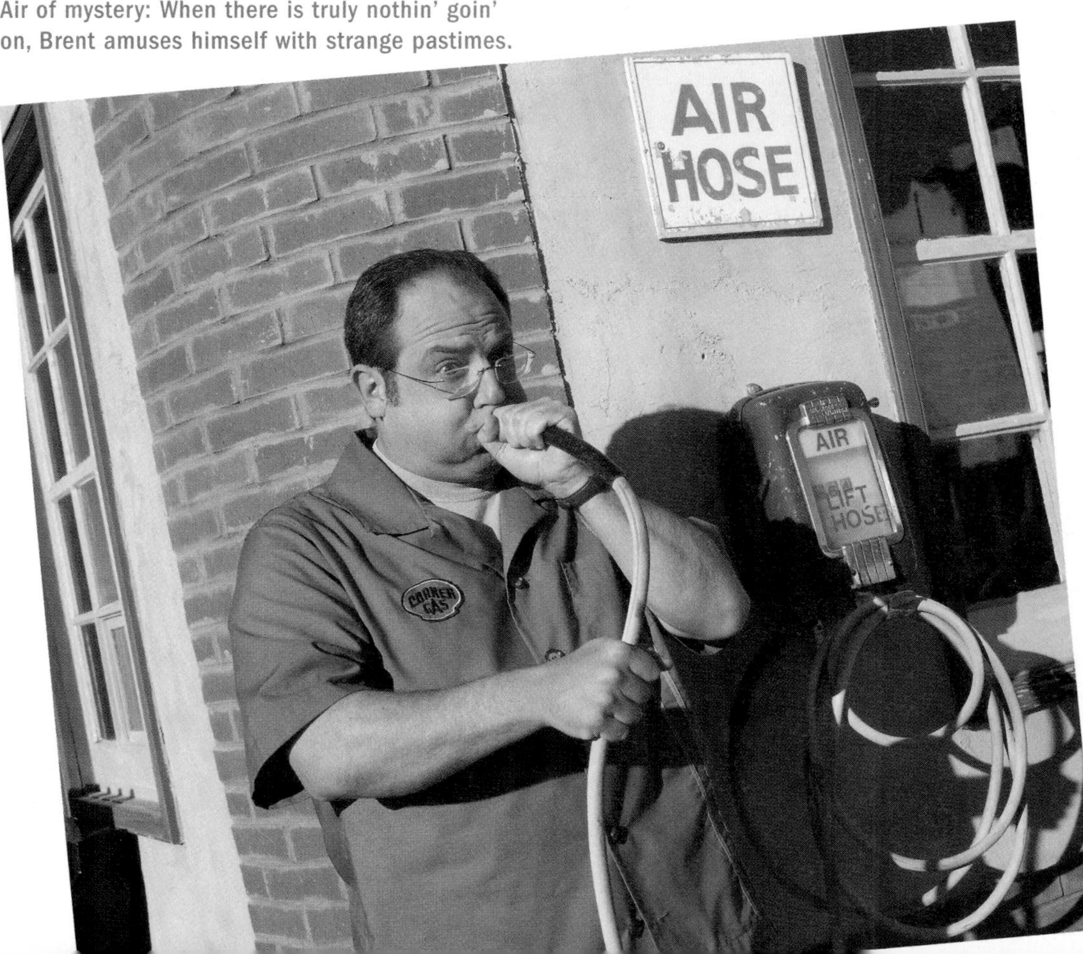

each character. The review process is repeated. More notes, more tweaks. A second draft follows, then—you got it—more notes and more tweaks.

When the script is about 80 percent complete, it goes to the story department. Everyone looks at it again, making sure the jokes are as good as they can be. At that point, the script moves on to the next step—referred to as "going to white"—and is sent out to all the various departments that need to know what's going on in order to get ready for filming. Props might have to be made, wardrobe and lighting worked out, special equipment ordered, sets built, and supporting actors cast.

It was in the early days of shooting Season 1, as the actors sat at the table reading their lines aloud, that the writers knew they were on to something really good. The cast members were laughing. And if they were laughing, maybe viewers watching this new, unknown show would too.

Let's not forget about the role direction plays in making episodes funny. A director is a lot like the conductor of an orchestra, pulling together all the creative elements of a show with precision timing. The director's tasks range from coaching actors with their delivery of lines to devising interesting camera angles for a scene. And directors add their own funny touches, though these may be more subtle than the lines the writers create. David Storey directs the majority of *Corner Gas* episodes, and while he doesn't claim to be a comedian, he understands humour well. For example, in Pilates Twist (Season 1), which David directed, Lacey is seen sitting on the floor, talking to those attending her Pilates class. She is shown in a close-up shot, then the camera moves around her so that viewers see the rest of the room. It's empty, with the exception of the lone participant, Davis. "I think that was an important moment," says David. "The writers witnessed first-hand how direction can create and add to the funny factor of the scripts."

Camerawork helped build humour once again in Season 1's Oh Baby. In this episode, viewers never see Tanner, Wanda's bratty six year old. How he looks is left to the imagination. Instead, many of the scenes are shot from Tanner's perspective. The camera is near ground level, peering up at Brent, his overwrought babysitter, while the house-of-horrors atmosphere is boosted by background music and the dim lighting in Wanda's place.

But above all else, it's the jokes that rule. If a line or a scene isn't funny, it may get chopped from the script. To ensure that the director, the one giving instructions to the actors, understands the subtleties and intentions of the jokes, the story editor explains them all, perhaps noting how a line should be delivered. One of the most satisfying moments for the writers—other than paycheque day—is seeing the cast do a table read of their script. It was in the early days of shooting Season 1, as the actors sat at the table reading their lines aloud, that the writers knew they were on to something really good. The cast members were laughing. And if they were laughing, maybe viewers watching this new, unknown show would too.

CAFE
THE
Ruby

Building the Buzz

A TV SHOW without an audience is like one hand trying to clap. Early on, before there was a set for The Ruby, or a cast, CTV and the producers of *Corner Gas* were sure that they had something unique. When the first season was wrapped, everyone felt without a doubt that the episodes had turned out as good as they had hoped. But would viewers tune in? Plenty of good-quality TV shows tank every year, destined to be remembered now and then merely as the answers to trivia questions.

With the first season complete and a few dollars left in the budget, Virginia, Brent, and David called CTV. "We wanted to spitball marketing ideas," recalls Virginia. CTV embraced the idea and

Fill 'er up: Brent Butt is in awe of Toronto prices in January 2004 during the Season 1 free gas promotion.

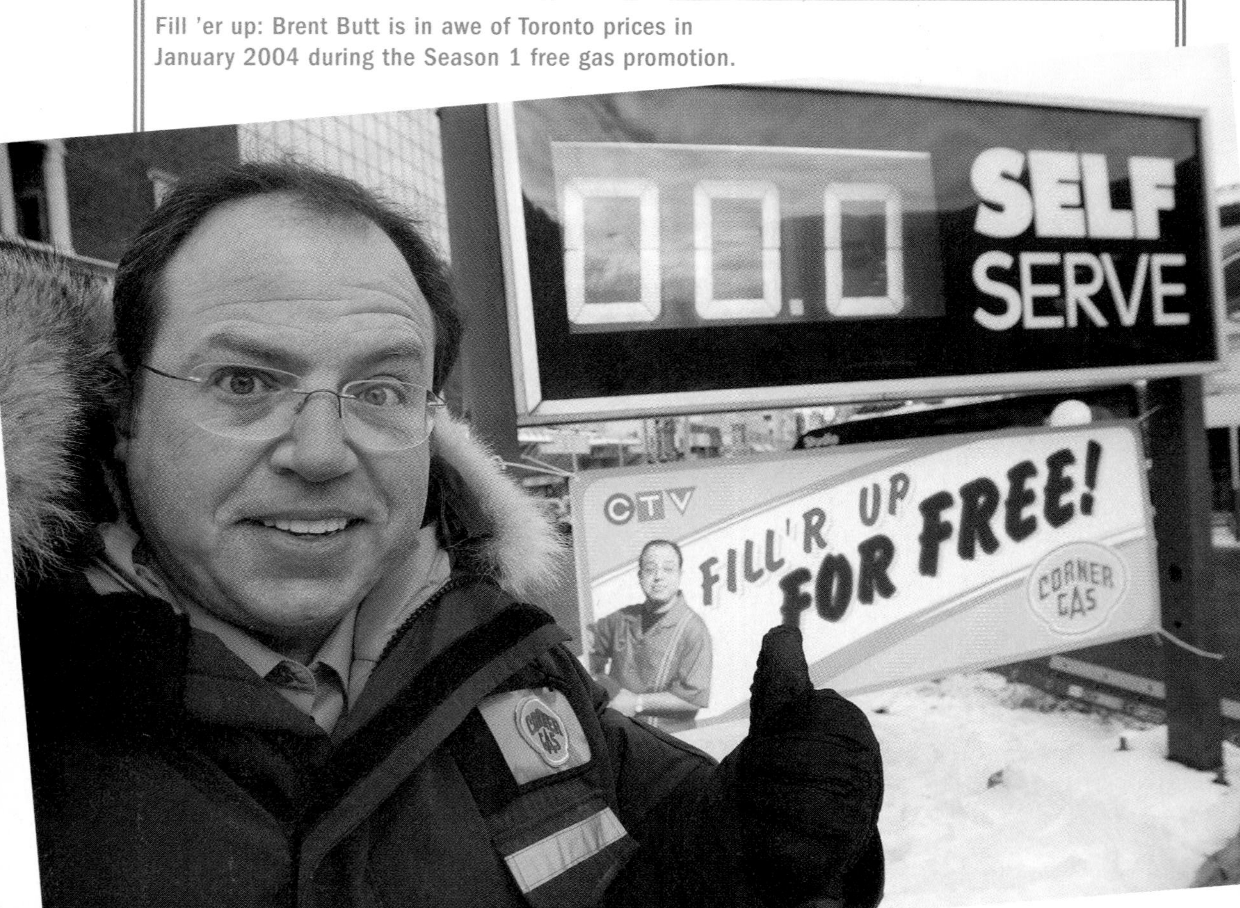

invited the team to screen the first two episodes with them in Toronto. Over 40 marketing, promotion, audience research, and production personnel shared ideas and their vision for *Corner Gas* ... and sure enough, a great launch idea surfaced.

What better way to promote a show that features a gas station than to give away gas? Those were the thoughts of CTV's Mike Cosentino, vice-president of programming communications, who came up with that crazy, yet savvy, idea. For the series debut, *Corner Gas* stars Brent Butt, Eric Peterson, and Nancy Robertson got up at five thirty on a frigid January morning to pump gas at the Canadian Tire at the intersection of Yonge Street and Davenport Road in Toronto. The first four hundred cars got their gas *gratis,* plus free coffee and doughnuts from Krispy Kreme. In return, drivers signed a pledge vowing that they'd check out the show, set to premiere on Thursday, January 22, 2004.

The next day, producers and the folks at CTV waited for the Nielsen ratings to roll in, city by city, from across the country. Trying to guess ratings is like trying to figure out how Hank's brain works. The thinking was that 500,000 viewers might tune in—a pretty respectable and optimistic number for a Canadian television show, especially one that was going to make its debut against a powerhouse hit like *Friends*. In the halls of CTV, everybody had a theory on how the show might do. There was even an office pool to guess how many viewers might watch the premiere of this baby comedy. No one came even close to getting it right.

The earliest figures were in the neighbourhood of 700,000, then climbed to 800,000. Then the numbers for western Canada came in. Over 1.1 million Canadians had watched the first episode of *Corner Gas,* Ruby Reborn. The top dog at CTV, Ivan Fecan, was quoted as saying, "We've got a live one here!" The execs dashed to their phones to relay the breaking news to every cast member and executive producer of the show. The reactions ranged from "shocked" and "mind-blowing" to "stunned." The media reviews for *Corner Gas* were overwhelming positive, even those from Canada's most cynical, seen-it-all television critics.

"I thought 500,000 was a fingers-crossed, pie-in-the-sky number," says Brent Butt. "We chalked it up to the great job that CTV did in promoting the show. I figured the number of viewers would die down, but it continued to build. People were talking about the show to friends and co-workers, giving their endorsement. It wasn't until Episode 3 or 4 that it struck me—*Corner Gas* was a hit."

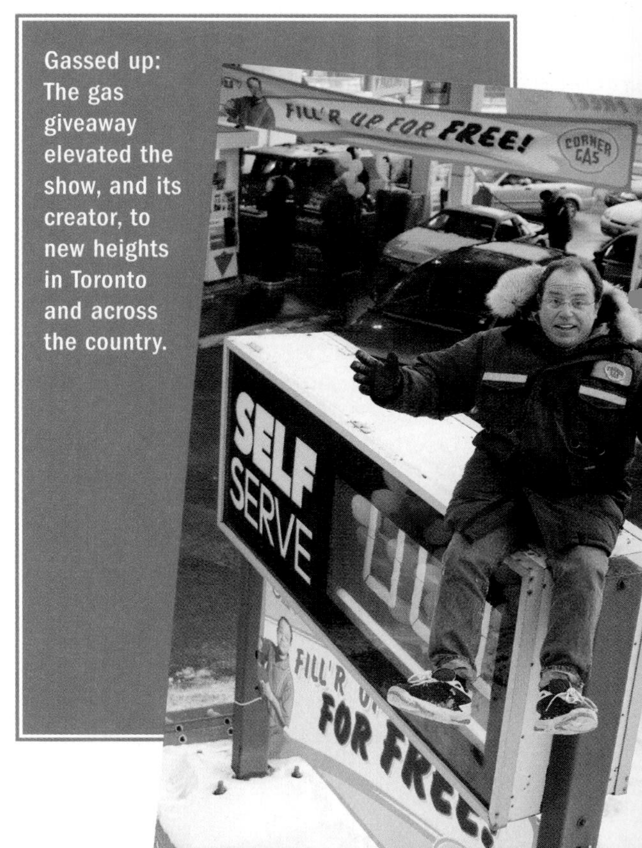

Gassed up: The gas giveaway elevated the show, and its creator, to new heights in Toronto and across the country.

Selected Awards and Nominations

As Walt Whitman once said, "If you done it, it ain't bragging."

2006 CANADIAN SCREENWRITING AWARDS:
Winner in the category—
Comedy and Variety, for the Season 3 episode Dog River Vice (Brent Butt, Paul Mather)

2006 GEMINI AWARDS: Nominee in the categories—
Best Comedy Program or Series
Best Ensemble Performance in a Comedy Program or Series
Best Writing in a Comedy or Variety Program or Series (Mark Farrell, Brent Butt, Paul Mather, Kevin White, for Season 3 episode Merry Gasmas)

2006 LEO AWARDS:
Best Music, Comedy, or Variety Program or Series (David Storey and Brent Butt, producers)
Best Direction in a Music, Comedy, or Variety Program or Series (Trent Carlson, for Security Cam, Season 2)
Best Performance or Host(s) in a Music, Comedy, or Variety Program or Series (Gabrielle Miller, for The Brent Effect, Season 2)

2005 CANADIAN COMEDY AWARDS: Winner in the categories—
Pretty Funny TV Direction—Series (David Storey)
Pretty Funny TV Male (Brent Butt)

2005 CANADIAN ENTERTAINMENT NETWORK AWARDS: Named—
Best Canadian DVD (English), for Season 1

2005 CANADIAN SCREENWRITING AWARDS:
Winner in the category—
Comedy and Variety

2005 DIRECTORS GUILD OF CANADA AWARDS:
Nominee in the category—
Outstanding Team Achievement in a Television Series—Comedy

2005 GEMINI AWARDS: Winner in the categories—
Best Comedy Program or Series
Best Interactive, for www.cornergas.com

2005 LEO AWARDS: Winner in the categories—
Best Music, Comedy, or Variety Program or Series
Best Direction in a Music, Comedy, or Variety Program or Series, for Season 1 episode I Love Lacey
Best Screenwriting in a Music, Comedy, or Variety Program or Series, for Season 1 episode Face Off (Brent Butt and Andrew Carr)
Best Performance or Host(s) in a Music, Comedy, or Variety Program or Series, for Season 1 episode Face Off (Gabrielle Miller)

2004 CANADIAN COMEDY AWARDS: Winner in the categories—
Pretty Funny TV Male (Brent Butt)
Pretty Funny TV Writing—Series (Mark Farrell, Brent Butt, Andrew Carr, Paul Mather)
Pretty Funny TV Direction (David Storey, Robert de Lint, Rob King, Henry Sarwer-Foner, Mark Farrell)

2004 DIRECTORS GUILD OF CANADA AWARDS:
Winner in the category—
Outstanding Team Achievement in a Television Series—Comedy

2004 GEMINI AWARDS: Nominee in the categories—
Best Comedy Program or Series
Best Ensemble Performance in a Comedy Program or Series, for Season 1 episode Face Off
Best Direction in a Comedy Program or Series (Rob King, for Season 1 episode Cousin Carl)
Best Writing in a Comedy or Variety Program or Series (Mark Farrell and Brent Butt, for Season 1 episode Tax Man)
Best Costume Design (Brenda Shenher, for Season 1 episode I Love Lacey)

2004 INTERNATIONAL EMMY AWARDS:
Nominee in the category—
Comedy

2004 *TV GUIDE* READERS' CHOICE AWARDS:
Voted—
Best New Canadian Show
Funniest Show on TV

Cast kudos: On the red carpet at the International Emmy Awards in New York.

DIESEL
0000
LITRES
LITRES

Meet the Cast

A television show is only as strong as its cast. In terms of *Corner Gas,* this ensemble of accomplished actors is as powerful as Spider-Man, the Incredible Hulk, and Luke Skywalker combined. Although the faces of the cast are well known now, the stories of how they became a part of the *Corner Gas* family aren't.

Meet the real people who make Hank, Oscar, Brent, Lacey, Emma, Wanda, Karen, and Davis so entertaining in every episode. Which actor is the most superstitious? Who despises fruit garnish? Who reveals their secret crush? Which one was traumatized by an encounter with a seal as a child? Who has hidden musical talents? All the dishy details are here, in this homage to the outstanding stars of *Corner Gas*.

Brent Butt

(BRENT LEROY)

JUST HOW MUCH ALIKE is the onscreen Brent to the off-screen version? "My character on the show is short and balding," explains Brent Butt, the creator and star of *Corner Gas*. "In my real life, I'm tall with a voluminous head of hair."

That's where the disparity ends. Brent Leroy and Brent Butt both have a sarcastic edge, softened by a heap of charisma and an Everyman, just-trying-to-earn-a-living kind of quality that so many identify with. It's what made Brent one of most roadworthy stand-up comics around, chalking up 15 years of gigs in cities and towns across Canada and beyond. With his track record as a comedian, Brent knew that people understood his brand of humour—one that oozes honesty and genuineness. But would it work in a TV series?

Brent was willing to try it and find out. His idea for a story that revolved around the antics of a motley crew of characters may have ended up on the big screen—*Corner Gas: The Movie* perhaps? Brent started to write a film script and thought it would be cool to set the story in small-town Saskatchewan. It had never been represented on screen. "As a kid, I remember that I was thrilled that, while watching cartoons one time, Daffy Duck said *Saskatchewan*. It was an exciting moment."

A good rule of thumb for all writers is to write what you know. Brent grew up in Tisdale, Saskatchewan, a town with a population of three thousand. He knew the life, the people. And with this particular script, it didn't really matter where the story was taking place. "But as I was writing, I realized it wasn't working as a movie. I tried to fix it, but I ended up abandoning it. Having Saskatchewan as a setting was working well though. I was coming up with some very funny stuff."

JUST THE FACTS CAREER HIGHLIGHTS

TV
- *Cold Squad* (2003)
- *Big Sound* (2001)
- *The X-Files* (1998)
- *Millennium* (1997)
- *The Kids in the Hall* (1993)

Film
- *Duets* (2000)

Kudos

2005 and 2004 Canadian Comedy Awards, Pretty Funny TV Male, for *Corner Gas*

2005 host of the Juno Awards, in Winnipeg

2004 Gemini Award nomination, Best Ensemble Performance in a Comedy Program or Series, for *Corner Gas*

2004 Leo Award, Best Screenwriting, for *Corner Gas*

2002 host of *Just for Laughs* in Singapore, part of the Asian tour

2001 Canadian Comedy Award, Best Male Stand-Up

2001 Represented Canada on World Comedy Tour in Australia

1988 Gemini Award nomination, Best Performance in a Comedy Program or Series for his *Comedy Now!* special *Funny Pants*

Rather than flush his work entirely, he switched gears and turned his idea into the premise for a TV show. He didn't expect much from it. "I wrote it just to purge the idea. Sometimes my ideas for things just get in the way, so I have to get them out of my head. I'd been thinking about the *Corner Gas* concept for a long time, so one day I just sat down and wrote it as a short treatment and outlined some of the characters. Then I didn't do anything with it."

In fact, the piece of paper it was typed on sat on the floor of his bedroom for a long time. That is, until his director buddy David Storey asked him if he had any ideas he could present to CTV bigwigs. You know the rest of the story from here. *Corner Gas* was officially born. At its centre were eight characters, each one with its own set of quirks. One of those characters was Brent, a TV version of Brent Butt, but with a few twists.

Everyone at some time or another has played the what-if game. For Brent, it was a question of, what if I wasn't a stand-up comedian and I had never left home? The answer? He might still be in a small

Stand and deliver: Brent wowed crowds across Canada during the *Corner Gas Live!* tour.

10 Things You Didn't Know About Brent Butt

1. He is fascinated with sasquatch.
2. In high school, he was voted valedictorian.
3. He was born August 3, 1966—the same day legendary comedian Lenny Bruce died.
4. He is anal-retentive about aligning things parallel with the edges of other things: "If there's a pencil lying on a table, I'll line it up with one of the sides of the table. I've done that all of my life," says Brent.
5. He has flat feet, "like a duck."
6. His all-time favourite performer is Dean Martin, followed closely by Jackie Gleason. "Basically, I like any performer who didn't feel the need to rehearse," Brent says.
7. As a kid, he loved to play any game that hurt—knuckles, shoulders. He also engaged in the occasional rock fight: "I had my head opened at least a couple of times."
8. He's been playing guitar since he was 13. Before he began guitar, he used to sneak upstairs and pull his brother John's banjo out from under the bed and pluck tunes.
9. He doesn't like seafood. "I don't mind fish. Like a regular fish. But lobsters and crabs and sea monkeys and squids ... no thanks."
10. He sings. "I'm terrible, but I don't care if I'm lousy at it. I sang the song 'The Rose' at two or three wedding receptions, despite my warning the bride and groom that I was going to ruin their wedding if they let me sing."

town pumping gas, hanging out with his pals, and saying funny stuff about nothing in particular. The reasonable facsimile Brent was also an only child. Flesh and blood Brent came from a family of seven children, where cracking jokes earned you a bit of attention and hopefully a few laughs.

These days, *Corner Gas* is getting Brent buckets of attention. Many of the letters he receives from fans say the same thing: The show can be watched and enjoyed by everyone in the family. "I like hearing that the most, because it takes me back to a time when my own family and I used to watch TV together. Though part of that was because we only had one television set."

When Brent is not acting, he's busy writing and overseeing scripts for *Corner Gas*. One of his favourite places to work is on an airplane. "My brain works really well there. Maybe it's the oxygen

FAVOURITE EPISODE

Rock On! (Season 2).

FAVOURITE BRENT LINE

"Dad's cranky. I saw him one time yell at a butterfly—called it a son of a bitch and told it to get out of his garden."
—from Tax Man (Season 1)

or something. I get very creative and focused, more so than when on the ground. One of my biggest problems in life is a lack of focus. Although it makes me good at what I do because I can bounce around from topic to topic, it can make life difficult, like when you're trying to do your taxes and you start thinking about fudge." Judging from the success of *Corner Gas,* there's no doubt that Brent Butt is flying high these days, even without a seat on an airplane.

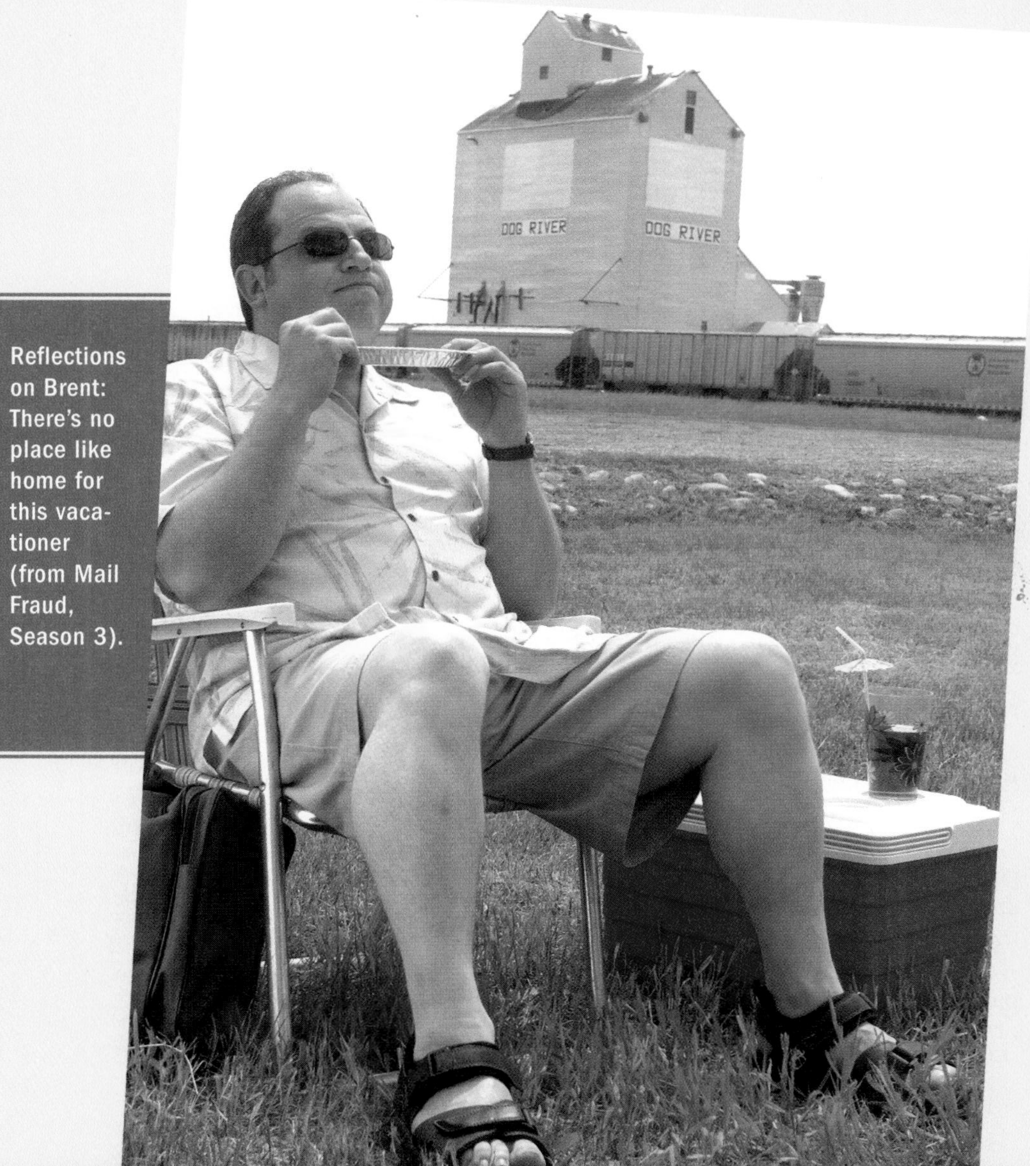

Reflections on Brent: There's no place like home for this vacationer (from Mail Fraud, Season 3).

Gabrielle Miller

(LACEY BURROWS)

A SNORKELLING TRIP to the Cayman Islands nearly derailed Gabrielle Miller's acting career. She was so taken with the beauty under the sea that she considered quitting the business to become a marine biologist. Luckily for the throngs of *Corner Gas* fans who adore Gabrielle's portrayal of hostess-with-the-mostest Lacey Burrows, her thoughts of spending her time in a water world were fleeting ones.

Like Lacey, Gabe, as her friends call her, is devoted to life in Dog River. "I love that my character ends up being the misfit in the middle of things that the locals consider rational," explains the Vancouver-based actor. "Having spent my whole acting life concentrating on drama, it's a real joy to be doing comedy. It's challenging because it has so many different levels to it. Timing is everything. It's like dancing."

Doing a bit of fancy footwork is nothing new to Gabe. She seemed to be born with the entertainment gene. At a young age, she took jazz, ballet, and, later on, salsa classes. The skills she learned came in handy later in life when she landed a TV commercial in which she had to cha-cha with a bowl of Cheezies perched on her head. It was her very first paid role.

At just eight years old, Gabe took her first acting lesson. "When I was a kid, we moved around a lot. I had this whole fantasy world in my head. I didn't feel comfortable expressing my imagination because I was really shy. Acting was so amazing because I got to put on characters and be in different life situations. It was freeing. After that first class, I thought, 'Oh, gosh. This is it.'"

Performing lead roles in her Montessori school plays, and participating in productions for a children's theatre group called The Green Thumb

FAVOURITE EPISODE

Slow Pitch (Season 3)—"It's rare that the cast gets to work together in scenes. The baseball storyline gave us all a chance to hang out."

FAVOURITE PROP

The coffee pot from The Ruby—"It has kind of connected with me."

FAVOURITE LACEY SCENE

Zealously chowing down forks of meatloaf (veggie version, of course) in an unladylike fashion at Oscar and Emma's house, in Season 2's Pandora's Wine.

Players, Gabe felt at home onstage. She made her film debut at age 18 in the movie *Digger,* a Canadian-made tear-jerker about a dying boy. Since then, she has chalked up more than 60 film and television roles to her credit, including an appearance on the TV show *Neon Rider,* where, coincidentally, she met the woman who would be her future *Corner Gas* co-star—Janet Wright.

Philosophical types might say that there are no accidents in life, just coincidences. But Gabe's arrival on the *Corner Gas* set certainly seemed serendipitous. "I was in the midst of moving. I came home to pack up my house and leave town. For some reason, I had to stay a few days longer than I had intended. That's when I got the call to come in and audition for the resident fish-out-of-water Lacey Burrows. I could have easily missed this opportunity."

Although she immediately loved the script and felt that she had done well in the audition with Brent Butt, Gabe wasn't about to get her hopes up. She had been down the unpredictable road of Canadian television before. But a couple weeks later, the call came: She had been chosen to play Lacey. Gabe was elated by the news.

Since the first episode, Lacey's comic struggles to fit into the quirky microcosm of Dog River have had viewers chuckling. It seems that everyone can relate to her being the sole square peg in a sea of round holes. Lacey is earnest in her efforts, whether it's taking on the town's pothole problems, wrangling a visit by the Snowbirds to The Ruby, or politely enduring protests over her coffee-refill policies. Lacey's uneasiness over being the odd woman out is one that many fans identify with: "I get lots of people telling me that they can relate to what Lacey is going through because they moved into a small town, too," says Gabe.

Perhaps one of the biggest fans of *Corner Gas* is Gabe herself. "I like that I can watch the finished episodes and still laugh at all of the jokes and their subtleties. The writing is so amazing, and I adore our cast. Our chemistry is so right and natural. Since day one in Regina, when I heard everyone read their lines out loud for the first time, I've thought, this is going to be fun."

JUST THE FACTS CAREER HIGHLIGHTS

TV
- ***Pasadena*** **(2005)**
- ***Robson Arms*** **(2005–)**
- ***Alienated*** **(2004)**
- ***Frasier*** **(2004)**
- ***The Outer Limits*** **(2002)**
- ***The Chris Isaak Show*** **(2001)**
- ***The X-Files*** **(1996, 1995)**

Film
- ***Love and Other Dilemmas*** **(2006)**
- ***Rupert's Land*** **(1998)**
- ***Digger*** **(1993)**

Kudos

Nominated for a total of nine awards, including—

2006 Leo Award winner, Music, Comedy, or Variety Program or Series: Best Performance or Host(s), for *Corner Gas* (The Brent Effect, Season 2)

2005 Leo Award winner, Music, Comedy, or Variety Program or Series: Best Performance or Host(s), for *Corner Gas* (Face Off, Season 1)

2004 Canadian Comedy Award nomination, Pretty Funny TV Female, for *Corner Gas*

2004 Gemini Award nomination, Best Ensemble Performance in a Comedy Program or Series, for *Corner Gas*

1999 Gemini Award nomination, Best Performance by an Actress in a Guest Role in a Dramatic Series, for *Da Vinci's Inquest*

10 Things You Didn't Know About Gabrielle Miller

1. She has a scar by her left eyebrow, the result of a childhood accident. She ran into a cutting board (the kind that slides out from a countertop) as she rushed into the kitchen to show her mom her clean plate, proof that she had earned dessert.
2. She is a confirmed vegetarian.
3. To keep in shape, she does yoga and runs. She can also pack a good punch, courtesy of her boxing training.
4. Her frequent sidekick is her pet Yorkie, Duncan.
5. Ironically, she worked at a gas station as a teen, sporting an ugly, brown polyester uniform.
6. Acting inspiration has come from greats like Elizabeth Taylor in *Who's Afraid of Virginia Woolf?* and Jessica Lange in *Frances*.
7. Guilty pleasures she reveals include shopping and watching *America's Next Top Model*.
8. As a kid, she made home-made perfume out of rose petals to sell to neigh-bours. Her entrepreneur-ial spirit appeared again when she started a housecleaning business as a teenager.
9. One of her passions is Vela Microboard, a British Columbia–based non-profit organization that supports people with disabilities—including her sister Shanti, who has cerebral palsy—to have autonomy and choices in their lives.
10. In Seasons 1 and 2 of *Corner Gas,* she could be spotted in between scenes wearing a bathrobe and gumboots—a comfy ensemble that became her trademark look for a while.

Bulletin bored: Lacey lays down the law in The Ruby about posting notes (Will and Brent, Season 3).

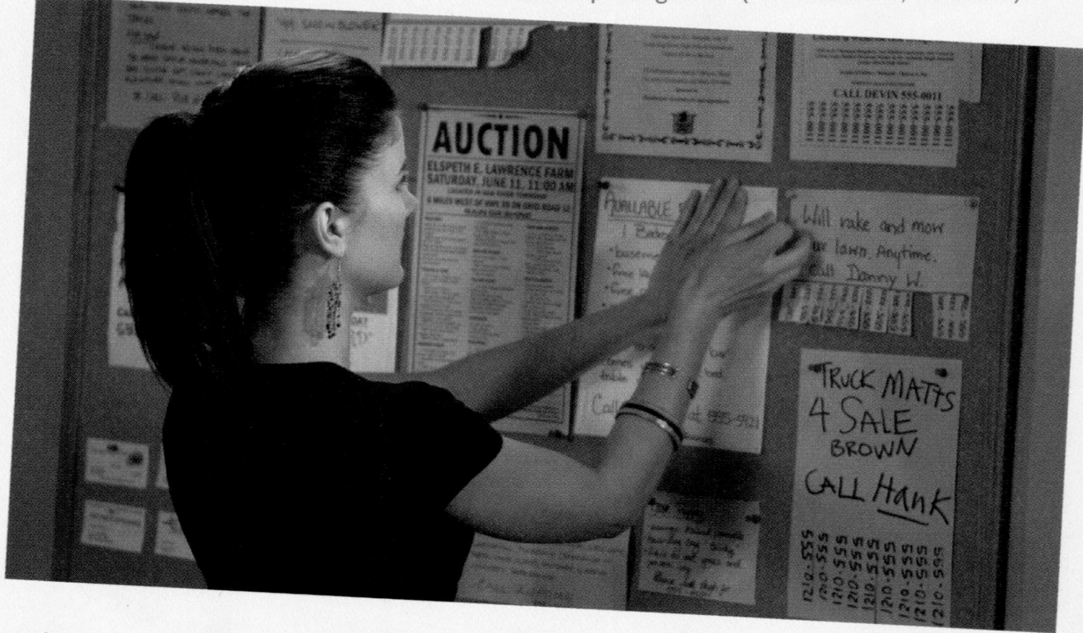

Tara Spencer-Nairn

(KAREN PELLY)

"I THOUGHT you'd be taller." That's the most common reaction *Corner Gas* fans have when they meet Tara Spencer-Nairn in person. When you think about it, that's a compliment to Tara and the huge way in which she fills the role of Dog River's newest member of the police department.

Tara is the first to admit that the line between Tara the actor and Karen the cop is pretty hazy. "It's so weird. I've never played a character for this long. She's just Karen. She's become such a part of me," says Tara. "As Karen, it's like a microscope is being placed over certain personality traits of my own."

One of those shared traits is an eager-beaver attitude, backed by equal parts of ambition and hard work. As a kid transplanted from Montreal and growing up in Vancouver, gymnastics served as an outlet for someone who hated to stay still for long. "It was my first love," says Tara. "I competed up until grade eight, and then I quit. And all of a sudden, I had all this excess energy that the teachers didn't know how to handle, so they put me in drama class."

Making the leap from floor mats to the stage felt right for Tara. "People ask me all the time when I decided to become an actor. I can't answer that question because it just happened. I just knew. When I was in the fourth grade, we were told to make a time capsule that would be opened in the year 2000. When my mom and I opened mine, there was my retainer, some gymnastic ribbons and medals, plus a letter I had written about what my life would be like. In it, I said that I would be an Olympic gymnast or a famous actress." Although it was Hank who claimed psychic ability in the Key to the Future episode in Season 3, perhaps Tara has the gift too.

JUST THE FACTS CAREER HIGHLIGHTS

TV

- ***Blue Murder*** **(2004)**
- ***Puppets Who Kill*** **(2004)**
- ***Relic Hunter*** **(2001)**
- ***The Outer Limits*** **(1998, 1997)**

Film

- ***Password*** **(2006)**
- ***Third Eye*** **(2006)**
- ***Waking Up Wally: The Walter Gretzky Story*** **(2005)**
- ***Rub & Tug*** **(2002)**
- ***New Waterford Girl*** **(1999)**

Kudos

2005 *TV Guide* named Tara as one of Canada's Top 10 Superstars of the Future

2004 Gemini Award nomination, Best Ensemble Performance in a Comedy Program or Series, for *Corner Gas*

2003 Canadian Comedy Award nomination, Pretty Funny Female Performance—Film, for *Rub & Tug*

1999 *New Waterford Girl,* her first major film debuted at the Toronto International Film Festival, then went on to earn seven Genie Award nominations

Tara attended Vancouver Film School in 1995 and soon after snagged small parts in well-known TV shows, including *The Outer Limits, Cold Squad,* and *Breaker High*. With her role in the critically acclaimed *New Waterford Girl* as a Bronx-raised teen who lands in small-town Nova Scotia, she went from invisible to invincible. A Canadian Comedy Award nomination for the indie flick *Rub & Tug* and landing a role on *Corner Gas* were just around the corner.

Now in her fourth season of playing über-keener Karen, Tara is finding more about her character to love. "She's quirky and goofy. Karen is like two different people—one in uniform and the other out." The chemistry that she has working alongside Lorne Cardinal (Davis Quinton) is something that Tara also digs. It's the real deal, even though the two didn't meet until two days before the cameras were set to roll. "He's the kindest, sweetest, and most genuine person I've ever met. He's been such

FAVOURITE EPISODES

Hook, Line and Sinker (Season 1); Air Show (Season 2).

FAVOURITE LINES

The Batman and Robin exchange with Davis in Block Party (Season 3):
Davis: "Batman doesn't keep secrets from Robin."
Karen: "Are you saying if we're Batman and Robin, I'm Batman ..."
Davis: "Dream on. I'm Batman."

Big wheelin': Karen wobbles her way during bike patrol (Air Show, Season 2).

10 Things You Didn't Know About Tara Spencer-Nairn

1. Her dad, John, was a racing car driver in Montreal. After retiring from racing, he was hired by Fiat and moved the family to Vancouver.
2. She has a real phobia of snakes, even fake ones.
3. Her guilty pleasure is York Peppermint Patties.
4. She's an avid fan of blue jeans, her closet boasting more than 30 pairs.
5. As kids, she and her sister would make home movies of little soap operas.
6. No matter where she travels, she brings along her favourite blankie.
7. She is in excellent physical shape, thanks to a regime that includes running, skipping rope, weight training, and Pilates.
8. As a creature of habit, she always has toast and peanut butter for breakfast, and popcorn almost every single night.
9. Her must-watch TV shows include *America's Next Top Model, Canadian* and *American Idol, King of the Hill, The Daily Show with Jon Stewart,* and the *CSI* series.
10. Elaine from *Seinfeld* is her most beloved TV character.

a great friend to me, such a positive person to have in my life," she says. Weirdly enough, Lorne and Tara also share the same birthday (January 6), and they're both left-handed.

Spending her days in polyester police garb has other advantages, too. Even in Toronto, where she makes her home, Tara is rarely recognized out of uniform. In fact, she rides on the Toronto subways without being spotted. But when's she standing next to her six-foot-tall co-star, the reaction is instant. Real-life cops and fans alike sing their praises and spout off favourite one-liners from the show.

Tara has been blown away by the success of *Corner Gas*. "All of us knew it was going to be a great show. At the first table read, we were in hysterics. It was just a question of whether people would watch. And they did. I'm just so honoured and privileged. I feel like we'll go down in Canadian history."

Nancy Robertson

(WANDA DOLLARD)

For every actor, auditions are a kind of prerequisite hell. At times, they can be ego-shredding experiences that leave you wondering whether you should consider another career. Fortunately, Nancy Robertson left her audition for *Corner Gas* feeling, if not exactly hopeful, at least positive.

"I got laughs in the right places, but I was already just thinking of it as just a nice experience," says the Vancouver native. "As an actor, you hear *no* a lot more than *yes*. I thought, I'll just let it go and forget about it. If I'm lucky, maybe they will think of me for some other future project."

The future came fast. The producers wanted Nancy to do a second read for the part of Brent's co-worker, Wanda Dollard, a well-educated brainiac with a razor-sharp mind and a tongue to match. And although they thought she was a good fit for the role, the official green light had to come from CTV's top brass. The wait was nerve-wracking for Nancy as she was put on hold for a role she knew instinctively was one with great possibilities. "Finally, my agent called and said, 'Pack your bags. You're going.' I was dumbfounded. I had already told myself that I didn't get the part. They phoned me on Monday and told me to be in Regina, for what would be a three-month stay, on Wednesday. I didn't even have time to absorb it all."

Gas stationed: Wanda takes a break.

Although Nancy had spent most of her life just a couple of provinces to the west, she had never been to Saskatchewan. She arrived at the Regina airport not knowing what to expect. There, a familiar face greeted her: that of Fred Ewanuick, her co-star from the hit indie film *The Delicate Art of Parking*. He had arrived the day before to start preparing for the role of Hank. "There was Fred standing in the airport, holding a sign that said, 'Nancy Robertson.' He was pretending that he didn't know me."

Fred's little prank went a long way toward making her feel at ease working on a brand-new show with cast mates she didn't know, and in an unfamiliar province to boot—a province that she learned to appreciate. Early on in the shooting of Season 1, Nancy was heading home on the long stretch of highway that leads from Rouleau to Regina. "I saw this big orange glow in the distance. I said to the driver, 'It looks like there's a fire over there.' There wasn't. It was the sun, sitting perfectly on the horizon. It was stunning."

Nancy quickly developed an appreciation for her cast mates as well. "Kudos to the people who did the casting. Although everyone was shy at first, after the first read-through of the script, there was an instant connection, an instant trust in the writing and in the show. It was a real bonding moment."

Over the course of three seasons, Nancy has also formed a real bond with her character, Wanda—someone who always has a ream of factoids to unfurl at any given moment, or helpful hints on correct grammar to unleash. "She has an insular way of being. She's very much in her head. Knowledge makes her tick. Wanda is book smart, not people smart. Someone like Emma is wise. You'd ask *her* for guidance, but not Wanda. She's intelligent, but she doesn't pay enough attention to people."

As a highly honed improv veteran who fine-tuned her skills performing with the award-winning Vancouver Theatre Sports League, Nancy is used to constantly being on her comedic toes. Working on *Corner Gas,* that talent and a love of physical comedy has come in handy. "If something feels right

JUST THE FACTS CAREER HIGHLIGHTS

TV
- *Dead Like Me* (2003)
- *Hollywood Off Ramp* (2000)
- *Los Luchadores* (2000)
- *Beggars and Choosers* (1999)
- *The New Addams Family* (1999)
- *The Eleventh Hour* (1997)

Film
- *Are We There Yet?* (2005)
- *Air Bud: Spikes Back* (2003)
- *The Delicate Art of Parking* (2003)
- *The Mall Man* (2003)

Kudos

2005 Canadian Comedy Award nomination, Pretty Funny TV Female, for *Corner Gas*

2005 Leo Award nomination, Feature Length Drama: Best Supporting Performance by a Female, for *The Delicate Art of Parking*

2004 Gemini Award nomination, Best Ensemble Performance in a Comedy Program or Series, for *Corner Gas*

2004 Leo Award nomination, Music, Comedy, or Variety Program or Series: Best Performance or Host(s), for *Corner Gas* (Face Off, Season 1)

for the character, we've got the freedom to give it a try," she says. Those scenes where you see Wanda leaping over the counter of Corner Gas and tearing after Hank are unscripted. "As an actor, you develop a sense of what fits and what doesn't."

Viewers have embraced Wanda and her unpredictable nature. Nancy shares her character's unpredictability. Just ask Gabrielle Miller, who answered a knock at her apartment door only to find Nancy in her pyjamas, playing a riff on her bass guitar. She had been taking lessons for Season 2's episode Rock On!, in which she and her band Thunderface reunite. "I really *was* playing the bass. It was one of my proudest moments. I just had to share it with someone."

Just like Wanda, Nancy possesses a special talent to captivate those around her with a hefty dose of charm and wit.

FAVOURITE EPISODE
Any in which all the cast gets to be in the same room together, including Face Off (Season 1), Slow Pitch (Season 2), and Hurry Hard (Season 2).

FAVOURITE WANDA ZINGER
"You choked like Tennessee Williams on a bottle cap."—from Bean There (Season 3)

FAVOURITE GUEST STARS
"I loved them all, from Jann Arden to Mark McKinney to The Tragically Hip and Colin James."

10 Things You Didn't Know About Nancy Robertson

1. Cakes and cupcakes take her to a happy place—"I could stare at a bakery window for hours," says Nancy. Fortunately, she also likes to go running.
2. She is devoted to watching the Food Network, though she doesn't cook. "I admire the amount of butter, mayonnaise, and cream Barefoot Contessa puts in her dishes."
3. She likes to annoy and amuse friends by spontaneously bursting into song in the middle of conversations. "I like to make up songs, mimic or mock musicals."
4. Her most exciting star encounter was with Joni Mitchell.
5. She is superstitious. While in a dressing room on set or at a theatre, she makes sure her shoes never leave the floor, even after she takes them off, fearing bad luck (a show-biz practice).
6. She is "filled with glee" when shopping for shoes, purses, and clothes.
7. She is short, just a smidgen over five feet tall, which comes as a surprise to some fans.
8. Friends tell her that she is the first to laugh at her own jokes, an endearing trait she shares with her *Corner Gas* character, Wanda.
9. Her main pet peeve in life is fruit touching the other food on her plate. She openly despises fruit garnishes.
10. On her celebrity meet-and-greet wish list are Emma Thompson, Judi Dench, Blythe Danner, and George Clooney (in her mind, he is the father of Wanda's son, Tanner).

Fred Ewanuick

(HANK YARBO)

IF YOU HAD ASKED Fred Ewanuick in high school what his future held, his answer would not have included acting. He had his sights set on spending his life on the road as a truck driver. Growing up in Port Moody, British Columbia, he loved hanging out at his grandfather's trucking company, surrounded by grease and diesel fumes.

Fred's parents weren't keen on their son's career choice so they pushed him into enrolling in college. Sadly, it didn't offer trucking courses. The only other thing there that appealed to Fred was the two-year theatre program. Fred had taken acting in high school as a no-sweat elective but soon discovered he liked the way portraying a character helped him overcome his shyness. But the class didn't turn out quite the way he had hoped. "I had a lousy experience in college," Fred recalls. "I think I was no good at school. My acting teacher didn't like me because she thought I was the class clown."

In just a year, he was out of the program and pondering his next move. Over the next couple of years, he lived a very Hank Yarbo–like existence, working a plethora of odd jobs—everything from serving nachos and orange pop at the local bingo hall to helping out a plumber fix leaks and declog drains. Through a friend of his mother's, Fred landed a job at Vancouver's Science World, where people with a theatre background were needed for kids' science shows. The job didn't stick, but some of the contacts he made did. Through a co-worker he met acting coach Shea Hampton. Working with her, Fred rekindled his love for acting. Trucking was out of the picture for good. Now he preferred to get lost in his roles rather than on the nation's highways.

The acting gigs came slowly at first but then picked up momentum as Fred snagged choice roles

JUST THE FACTS CAREER HIGHLIGHTS

TV
- *Robson Arms* (2005–)
- *Da Vinci's Inquest* (2003, 2001)
- *Dark Angel* (2001–2002)

Film
- *Black Eyed Dog* (2006)
- *Love and Other Dilemmas* (2006)
- *Young Triffie's Been Made Away With* (2006)
- *Just Friends* (2005)
- *A Guy Thing* (2003)
- *The Delicate Art of Parking* (2003)
- *The Santa Clause 2* (2002)

Kudos

2005 Gemini Award nomination, Best Ensemble Performance in a Comedy Program or Series, for *Corner Gas*

2004 International Comedy Film Festival of Peniscola, Best Actor, for *The Delicate Art of Parking*

Keep on truckin': Hank relaxes in his beloved pickup.

in films like *The Santa Clause 2, A Guy Thing,* and the award-winning comedy *The Delicate Art of Parking*. He racked up impressive TV credits, too, with *Da Vinci's Inquest, Dark Angel,* and *Selling Innocence*. He was hooked. "It's like being a kid again," Fred explains. "I get to pretend. It's a bit of a rush, a natural high."

Those feelings of reverting to childhood would come in handy playing Hank Yarbo, a role he auditioned for twice but wasn't too hopeful of getting. Not because he didn't believe in his talents, but this was Canada after all, and steady work could be as rare as a Gordie Howe rookie-year hockey card. When Fred's agent told him the role was his, he felt, he said, "like I had won the lottery."

10 Things You Didn't Know About Fred Ewanuick

1. His nickname is Derf (Fred spelled backwards).
2. As a kid, he was traumatized while swimming in the ocean by the sudden appearance of a seal just a few feet from him. He still doesn't like swimming where there are creatures because of the prevailing fear that something may grab him from underneath. Yes, he did see *Jaws*.
3. He loves buying DVDs. His top three all-time favourite flicks are *Slap Shot, Cool Hand Luke, and The Graduate*.
4. He can't watch a movie without eating Nibs.
5. In his early 20s, he cut up his leg badly, the result of a run-in with a fish tank at home. He was off his feet for almost a year.
6. One of his hidden talents is crocheting—something he learned out of boredom while shooting a film.
7. During a hiatus from *Corner Gas*, he drove across Canada with his fiancée, Toresa (a ballet teacher), and their dog, Chloe (a Lab cross).
8. He makes a decent vegetarian lasagne and no-meat version of his mom's Italian sausage soup.
9. He's superstitious. He carries a piece of wood with him so that he can knock on wood whenever he needs to.
10. Sports are his passion—hockey, lacrosse, and ultimate.

It was great to have a steady paycheque, but the biggest thrill was being able to play the lovable Hank, the man-child about town (Dog River, that is) who devotes his days to hanging around Corner Gas and amusing his boyhood friend, Brent Leroy, with his knuckleheaded schemes and dim-witted theories. Cerebrally challenged or not, Hank has struck a chord with viewers.

"Hank's not too bright, but he does have a good heart and tries to help. He just doesn't go about it the right way. He's a good guy, and it seems that everyone knows someone like him," says Fred. "People connect with his innocence and his honesty. It's easy to get up in the morning and go to work when you're portraying a guy like this." From the viewers' point of view, he's an easy character to adore, too.

FAVOURITE EPISODES

Face Off (Season 1); Hook, Line and Sinker (Season 1); and Rock On! (Season 2)—"All of these episodes show different aspects of Hank."

FAVOURITE GUEST STAR

The Tragically Hip (Rock On!, Season 2).

Lorne Cardinal

(DAVIS QUINTON)

ALL EYES turned toward Lorne Cardinal as he sat in a Toronto restaurant—not so unusual for the well-known Canadian actor who plays Officer Davis Quinton on *Corner Gas*. Except at this time, he hadn't yet appeared on air in that role. Lorne was attracting attention because he was laughing. His fellow patrons couldn't help but wonder why this handsome man sitting alone was chuckling.

What they didn't know was that he was reading scripts for the show's first two episodes. "I couldn't help it. They were just so funny," Lorne recalls. "The most brilliant comedic brains in Canada were working on the show, giving you amazing material."

The dirt road to Dog River has its share of potholes for the acclaimed theatre and television actor. Born in Sucker Creek, Alberta, Lorne was 26 years old when he decided to become an actor. He had returned to school in his early 20s, attending Cariboo College in Kamloops, British Columbia, where he chose an Introduction to Acting class for what he thought would be an easy credit. Right off the bat, he was hooked. "I had an incredible teacher, Dr. David Edwards. He turned my life around. He saw that I had some talent and he encouraged me to get more training. This was my calling. I knew I had found something."

Off Lorne went to the University of Alberta to undertake a bachelor of fine arts. In the midst of his studies, he got a call from the TV series *North of 60* to audition for a lead role. He said no: He was committed to furthering his education.

His dedication has paid off. After racking up an impressive list of stage and screen credits, which ended up including a recurring role on *North of 60,* Lorne found himself at the *Corner Gas* audition. He felt cautiously optimistic about landing the role of

FAVOURITE EPISODE

Security Cam (Season 2), the one in which Davis gets a TASER gun.

FAVOURITE DAVIS LINE

"Good hustle out there guys … anyone seen my pancreas?"—said during a time out in the hockey game, in Face Off (Season 1)

Davis. By the time he had finished the audition, all the producers were grinning. Shooting was to begin in two weeks. But the start date slipped by, and still no call. Lorne was distraught about not getting hired. But like any experienced actor, he brushed off the dust from his slightly wounded ego and took another job. In Lorne's case, it was *The Storyteller's Bag,* a production that recounts Ojibwa stories, accompanied by a chamber music ensemble. Then he got a call from his agent: The producers wanted him—and fast. They hoped he could be on a plane for Regina that evening. Lorne couldn't do it, not until he had finished the project he was working on. Luckily, the producers agreed to wait a week or so until Lorne wrapped *The Storyteller's Bag*. He did so, at 11 o'clock in the morning, and by 4 o'clock that afternoon, he was on a plane headed from his current home in Ontario to Regina.

The next day he met his onscreen partner in crime prevention, Karen Pelly (Tara Spencer-Nairn), walking to set. It was the first time they had crossed paths, but their connection was immediate. Lorne had admired Tara's acting in *New Waterford Girl* and was thrilled to have her as his sidekick. "She's a real sparkplug," he says. "We work really well together. It's lucky. The character of Davis clicks because of his partner. The two go hand in hand."

Portraying the committed cop who likes to go all out no matter what he does, whether it be planning nuptials for Oscar and Emma or preparing for the police physical exam, Lorne brings the complexities of his character to life. Davis is a manly man who is confident enough to wear a pink shirt to a wedding and join in a Pilates class.

The richness of his character isn't lost at all on *Corner Gas* fans—even the ones in uniform. After a RCMP rehearsal for the Queen's visit to Edmonton, an event Lorne was co-hosting, Lorne was swarmed by RCMP officers wanting to shake his hand and to tell him how much they enjoyed the show. Even an ex–chief of police gave him his blessing. For Lorne, this kind of fame and recognition are "just gravy." His main goal? "I want to tell great stories with incredible words. I just want to be an actor."

JUST THE FACTS CAREER HIGHLIGHTS

TV

- ***Moccasin Flats*** (2005, director)
- ***Distant Drumming: A North of 60 Mystery*** (2004)
- ***renegadepress.com*** (2004, actor and director)
- ***Relic Hunter*** (2002)
- ***Blackfly*** (2001)
- ***Jake and the Kid*** (1995)

Film

- ***Insomnia*** (2002)

Theatre

- ***Dry Lips Oughta Move to Kapuskasing*** (2004)
- ***The Artshow*** (2004)
- ***Time Stands Still*** (director, 2003)
- ***Royal Hunt of the Sun*** (2002)
- ***Thunderstick*** (director, 2002)
- ***fareWell*** (2001)
- ***Black Elk Speaks*** (1994)

Kudos

2005 University of Alberta Alumni Horizon Award

2004 Gemini Award nomination, Best Ensemble Performance in a Comedy Program or Series, for *Corner Gas*

1999 and 1998 Jessie Award nominations, Best Supporting Actor, for *Only Drunks and Children Tell the Truth*

1999 Sterling Award nomination, Best Supporting Actor, for *High Life*

1995 First Americans in the Arts nomination, Best Supporting Actor, for *Tecumseh: The Last Warrior*

10 Things You Didn't Know About Lorne Cardinal

1. He loves to golf whenever he has the chance.
2. He has a kitty named Homer and has been known to refer to friends and colleagues as "cats."
3. He once worked in a recycling plant, and he also planted trees.
4. Rice pudding is one of his favourite comfort foods.
5. He's seriously crazy about rugby, a sport he played competitively with the Strathcona Druids—the first Aboriginal person ever to do so.
6. Helping youth is one of his passions. He often speaks to students about the importance of education, and he is active in charity events in and around Regina.
7. He plays a wicked harmonica.
8. He's an enthusiastic collector of Native art.
9. He can often be found with his nose in a book. He counts Thomas King among his favourite authors.
10. His number one pet peeve is tardiness.

Dapper Davis: He gives men in uniform a good name.

Eric Peterson

(OSCAR LEROY)

SPOILER ALERT: Don't read the following if you want to believe that Eric Peterson is a lot like his onscreen character, Oscar the grouch. Truth is, Eric isn't much like him at all. The fact that many fans blur the line between fact and fiction is a testament to Eric's finesse as an actor.

When he learned that the role of Oscar was up for grabs, Eric knew he had to have it. Not only did the writing of *Corner Gas* scripts captivate him, but there was an instant understanding of the complex layers that make up this cantankerous, yet endearing, character. "It's the only audition where at the end of it, I addressed the producers and said, 'You must give me this part. It would be a huge mistake if you didn't. I am this guy.'"

They agreed with him. He was cast alongside Janet Wright, his long-time friend from the University of Saskatchewan, in Saskatoon, where he fell into acting. "It's a huge treat to work with Janet," says Eric, who was born in Indian Head, about 65 kilometres east of Regina. "I can't overstate my admiration of Janet's talents. She's an incredibly intelligent woman. And she's striking looking, too. You'd never miss Janet Wright in a room. She's a very vivid person. We're compatible souls. We worry, rejoice, have fun, and laugh at the same things. It makes us good buddies."

Despite the clashes between Oscar and Emma, they too are friends. "Emma is always 10 steps ahead of Oscar. He's not very mature, in a way. That's why so many of my fans are eight-year-old boys. There's a part of Oscar that is still that age. He wants things his way and he thinks everyone but himself is a jackass," says Eric. Incidentally, when Eric uttered his first *jackass,* he had no idea that it would become Oscar's infamous catchphrase. "It

JUST THE FACTS CAREER HIGHLIGHTS

TV

- *Trudeau II: Maverick in the Making* (2005)
- *This Is Wonderland* (2004–2006)
- *Blue Murder* (2004)
- *Puppets Who Kill* (2002)
- *Trudeau* (2002)
- *Da Vinci's Inquest* (1998)
- *Touched by an Angel* (1998)
- *La Femme Nikita* (1997)
- *Street Legal* (1987–94)

Theatre

- *Half Life* (2005)
- *The Dishwashers* (2005)
- *Clout* (2001)
- *Hysteria* (2000)
- *Billy Bishop Goes to War* (1978–82, then again for a 20th anniversary reunion in 1998)

Kudos

2004 Canadian Comedy Award nomination, Pretty Funny TV Male, for *Corner Gas*

2004 Gemini Award nomination, Best Ensemble Performance in a Comedy Program Series, for *Corner Gas*

continued on next page

sort of developed over the course of Season 1. *Jackass* is so much fun to say. It's actually a clean word. I love it."

Just as much a part of Oscar is his wardrobe, notably his silver belt buckle and his green Dog River cap with a white embroidered oil derrick. His colleagues describe Eric as a perfectionist. That trait could explain his search for the perfect hat for Oscar. It had to be right—something an older Saskatchewanian would wear. For his hat, Eric envisioned one that a farmer might wear when coming into the city with his wife to shop at the mall. Then, working with the costume department, he was able to choose the hat and figure out how it should be worn—angled and sitting back on his head a bit, as though a prairie wind had blown it slightly askew. It has turned into a signature look that is pure Oscar.

Such attention to detail goes into every aspect of making Oscar funny. Even his irrational anger over small things is laughable and not taken terribly seriously, other than by Oscar himself. That sense of indignant rage is something that Eric can relate to: "Oscar is a creation of Brent Butt and the writers, but when I am doing him, I think of my own dad. He didn't get mad very often, but when he did ..." It's a quality that strikes a chord with many folks. "I get people coming up to me and, with a sense of great confidentiality, they whisper, 'You're just like my husband,' or 'my Uncle George.' It's incredibly pleasing to me as an actor that people do find Oscar Leroy so familiar. He was recognizable to me, too. This guy is totally plausible."

Not only is Oscar credible, he's undeniably hilarious. Oddly enough, Eric's TV resumé was somewhat light on comedy: "I'd never done any on TV. It's a bit harder than drama because comedy is so precise. There's a certain latitude with drama, but with comedy, timing is crucial." But Eric loves this challenge. "It's great to spend your day preoccupied with making something as funny as possible. It's a healthy way to live."

JUST THE FACTS CAREER HIGHLIGHTS

Kudos 1995, 1994, and 1993 Gemini Award nominations, Best Performance by a Lead Actor in a Continuing Dramatic Role, for *Street Legal*

1992, 1989, and 1987 Gemini Awards, Best Performance by a Lead Actor in a Continuing Dramatic Role, for *Street Legal*

1978 Starred in *Billy Bishop Goes to War* in Vancouver, then toured with the show internationally, making stops in London's West End, Broadway, and at the Edinburgh Festival

FAVOURITE EPISODE

Pilates Twist (Season 1), in which Oscar builds his own coffin.

RUNNERS-UP

Picture Perfect (Season 3), showcasing Oscar's bitter feelings about garden gnomes; Telescope Trouble (Season 3), which has Oscar and Emma cruising around town in a RV.

FAVOURITE LINE

"Can't just leave them there. That's pants. It'd be a waste. A waste of pants."—from Lost and Found (Season 2)

10 Things You Didn't Know About Eric Peterson

1. His father was an entomologist (an insect expert) who studied a particular type of tree-munching beetle.
2. Feel free to address Eric as Doc Peterson. He was awarded an honorary degree, doctor of letters, from the University of Saskatchewan.
3. He has a twin sister named Barbara who runs the Deerhaven Bed and Breakfast in Katepwa Beach, near Fort Qu'Appelle, Saskatchewan.
4. His guilty pleasure? "I watch *Corner Gas* and still laugh. It's great fun to think back to the first read-through of the script," says Eric.
5. He has snagged a number of Gemini Awards—one of which he uses as a doorstop.
6. His newest passion is his 16-foot-long sailboat, *The Molly Kate,* named after his two daughters.
7. He has a "strong, basic attachment" to vanilla ice cream.
8. One of his most prized possessions is the original Arts and Crafts chair used on the set of *Billy Bishop Goes to War*.
9. His favourite TV reality show is hockey.
10. He's a proud bookworm, reading and rereading novels by authors John le Carré and Ian McEwan.

Pant waist: Oscar's garbage picking pays off (Lost and Found, Season 2).

Janet Wright

(EMMA LEROY)

In describing their *Corner Gas* co-star, colleagues have called Janet Wright "a member of Canada's acting royalty." She has been a fixture onstage, and on movie and television screens, for more than 40 years.

It's fitting, then, that the role for which she has received the most attention is Emma Leroy, Dog River's resident matriarch and frequent voice of reason. "I never wanted to be famous," says Janet, who emigrated from England as a child. "It was okay for me not to be recognized at all. Then all of a sudden, after the first season aired, people started coming up to me and congratulating me on the show. It was shocking, and it still is, even after three seasons."

The recognition may seem surprising to her because, once she began acting, Janet felt that it was something she was always meant to do. When she was a child in her new home in Saskatoon, her mom often bought long-playing records of current Broadway musicals. Janet and her younger sister, Susan, would learn all the words and sing all the roles to classics like *West Side Story.* When Janet finished high school, she didn't know what to do with herself. "I went to Vancouver and decided to be an actor because it just seemed like an easy thing to do." An understandable choice, since acting and performing were so familiar to her, having been a part of her life growing up.

Now her acting family includes talents like Eric Peterson, who plays her lovable curmudgeon of a husband, Oscar. The affection the two have for one another is real. They have been friends for more than 35 years. "I met Eric when he was 18. He was so cute. I had a crush on him. He was acting then, too, and he was a star among our group of friends."

FAVOURITE GUEST STAR
Shirley Douglas—"I had a ball with her."

FAVOURITE LINE
(To a naked Oscar): "I didn't think you were holding a wrinkly purse."—from Poor Brent (Season 2)

FAVOURITE EPISODE
Oh Baby (Season 1), in which Emma saves the day when Brent babysits, by using open-ended threats with darling Tanner.

Although they would go separate ways to pursue their careers, Eric and Janet seemed destined to be together again. When her agent called her to tell her about a Canadian comedy that was being shot on location in Saskatchewan, her reaction was, "Oh my God. What's this?" As she read the script for *Corner Gas* and "laughed her head off," Janet realized it was something special.

Then came news that she would be auditioning with another Canadian actor who was vying for the role of her impetuous, childlike spouse, Oscar. It was Eric. And naturally, the chemistry between the two old friends was pure magic. "It was so easy from the very first day we worked together. He has a tremendous affection for women. He prefers the ballsier type of woman. He's not intimidated. He is a kind and caring guy, and has the greatest smile. I've never told him this, but I also love the way he walks."

With these kind of warm and fuzzy feelings for one another, their portrayal of an onscreen couple is entirely believable, even when Oscar is at his grouchiest. "I get lots of women telling me that they have husbands just like him," explains Janet. "In some ways, Emma and Oscar have the ideal marriage. He might drive Emma crazy, but they handle things with a bit of humour. They still sit down at the table and have a meal together. If one lost the other, they'd be completely lost."

For Janet, a character like Emma, who is often the epitome of calm even in the middle of a stormy situation, is a joy to play. "Emma is a very cool woman. She's a rock. She seems very happy with her life."

Away from the wackiness of Dog River, Janet feels right at home onstage, having directed and performed with the best theatre companies in Canada. During the most recent hiatus from *Corner Gas*, she returned to her roots, playing the British wife of a banker in the dark comedy *Absurd Person Singular*, produced by the Vancouver Arts Club Theatre Company. "Being in front of a live audience again was really great. I hadn't done that in years."

Still, her heart belongs to *Corner Gas*. "It's a warm place to come home to," says Janet. "In my own life, I relate to humour. It gets me through the day."

JUST THE FACTS CAREER HIGHLIGHTS

TV

- *Kingdom Hospital* (2004)
- *Monk* (2002)
- *The Chris Isaak Show* (2002)
- *Dark Angel* (2001)
- *Lexx* (2001)
- *Due South* (1998)
- *Street Legal* (1994, 1993)
- *The Beachcombers* (1987)
- *King of Kensington* (1979)

Film

- *Love and Other Dilemmas* (2006)
- *Betrayed* (2003)
- *Chasing Cain* (2001)
- *The Perfect Storm* (2000)
- *Bordertown Café* (1993)
- *McCabe and Mrs. Miller* (1971)

Kudos

2006 Star in the B.C. Entertainment Hall of Fame

2004 Gemini Award nomination, Best Ensemble Performance in a Comedy Program or Series, for *Corner Gas*

2003 Gemini Award, Best Performance by an Actress in a Featured Supporting Role in a Dramatic Program or Mini-Series, for *Betrayed*

1992 Genie Award, Best Performance by an Actress in a Leading Role, for *Bordertown Café*

10 Things You Didn't Know About Janet Wright

1. She once had a job working at a music store in Regina. She pretended she could read sheet music, and recommended music to customers based solely on the appeal of its title.
2. Her birthday is March 8, making her a Pisces.
3. She acted alongside screen legend Katharine Hepburn in the 1988 made-for-TV movie *Laura Lansing Slept Here*.
4. Her addiction is television. She has a TV set in almost every room of her Vancouver apartment. She loves *Canadian* and *American Idol, Dr. Phil*, and *The Oprah Winfrey Show*, plus news programs. She even studies her lines with the television on in the background.
5. Two of her all-time top flicks include the 1940 version of *Rebecca,* and *Now, Voyager*—"I'm a bit of a sap," says Janet.
6. She's an avid gardener, and loves roses.
7. When she's not acting, she relaxes onboard her 28-foot-long boat, *Starlight Drifter*, named by her granddaughter.
8. She collects ceramic pigs—"They make me laugh."
9. Her Genie Award for *Bordertown Café* accidentally fell 22 storeys from her apartment window. Miraculously, the statuette suffered only minor injuries.
10. She has shed more than 20 kilograms by eating healthier and limiting the white flour in her diet. She treats herself during the *Corner Gas* food scenes in which she enjoys macaroni and cheese with wieners.

Pants fever: Emma is a snappy dresser with great fashion sense.

Love and marriage: Oscar and Emma have a special connection, as do Eric Peterson and Janet Wright.

Episode Guide

Think you know *Corner Gas* fairly well? Watched every episode? Savoured each zippy quip? Take a closer look at your favourite shows in this exclusive look beyond your television screen into what really goes on in Dog River—and there's plenty, from props and plots, to cameras and cameos.

Through more than 30 interviews with the cast and crew of *Corner Gas,* secrets are revealed—inside jokes, pop culture allusions, milestones, off-camera moments, and more. Rewind to the best jokes and one-liners, keep track of how many times you hear *jackass* uttered and just how many cups of coffee appear in each caffeine-fuelled episode. It's all here in this dandy, handy episode guide. Read on ...

Season 1
Episode 1

First aired: **January 22, 2004**
Writers: **Brent Butt and Mark Farrell**
Director: **David Storey**

18

Notice the *Decoy* movie poster on the wall of the Corner Gas store? This low-budget action movie from 1985 starred Peter Weller (*RoboCop*) and was shot in Saskatchewan. Among its crew was a young special-effects assistant named Jay Robertson, now the props master on *Corner Gas*.

Ruby Reborn

THE TOWN OF DOG RIVER, Saskatchewan, is in an uproar. There's change afoot and no one is happy about it. Brent Leroy, who has taken over the corner gas station from his father, rankles Oscar's nerves by introducing video rentals. Meanwhile, Hank Yarbo is highly suspicious of the new girl in town from Toronto (Lacey Burrows), who is now running the coffee shop next door, and of her fancy big-city ways. Rebellion and the smell of coffee are in the air.

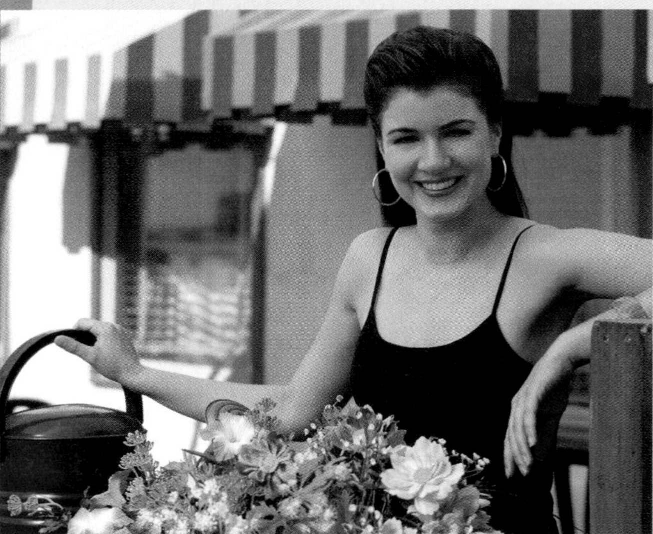

Bloom with a view: Lacey brings a woman's touch to The Ruby.

HOWLER HIGHLIGHTS

- Moose Jaw Gets NBA Franchise
- Big City Woman Destroys Landmark
- Death from Above (about a rock from space that killed one of Farmer Anderson's chickens)

Opening act: Brent and Hank treat a customer (Mark Farrell, left) to some old-fashioned sarcasm.

ON A ROLE

Mark Farrell, the man who drives up to Corner Gas in the opening scene, does triple duty as actor, writer, and supervising producer on this episode.

REALITY CHECK

- Oscar and Emma Leroy's house number is 717, Brent's homage to a house in Saskatoon where he and his classmates would crash after a night of partying.
- In one take, where Brent is talking to newscaster Dan Matheson, a fly was buzzing around Brent's head. As writer and supervising producer Mark Farrell explains, "We didn't use that take, even though it was funny. It was too distracting. There are a million ways to derail a joke."

STYLE ON FILE

Janet Wright (Emma) so loved the tiger-print sweater she wore in this episode that she borrowed it for her personal wardrobe.

WATCH FOR IT

In Season 1, budget restrictions made it necessary for Brent Butt and David Storey to share a rental car. Their blue vehicle got some screen time, appearing in the first scene of the season and in the last one.

TOP PROP

Visitors to the Rouleau set develop eye strain looking for the place where Officer Karen Pelly parked her police cruiser. The surveillance bush that marked the spot didn't exist. Lead props guy Roger Roscoe, lying on his belly in the tall grass, swayed fig tree branches in a fake prairie wind.

- Over 1.2 million viewers tune in for the show's premiere. And the producers thought they were being optimistic when they projected a figure in the neighbourhood of 500,000!
- The much despised town of Wullerton—*spit*—is mentioned for the first time.
- Brent scarfs down a chili cheese dog for the first, but definitely not the last, time in the series.

QUIPS AND QUOTES

From the first scene of the series:

Brent: "Want me to fill it up?"

Man: "Sure. You know, I've never driven across Saskatchewan before."

Brent: "Well, you still haven't really. About half way to go yet."

Man: "Sure is flat."

Brent: "How do you mean?"

Man: "You know, flat. Nothing to see."

Brent: "What do you mean, like topographically? Hey, Hank, this guy says Saskatchewan is flat."

Hank: "How do you mean?"

Brent: "Topographically, I guess. Says there's nothin' to see."

Hank: "There's lots to see. Nothin' to block your view."

Brent: "There's lots to see. Nothin' to block your view. Like the mountains back there. They're, uh ... er, what the hell? I could've sworn there was a big mountain range back there. Juttin' up into the sky all purple and majestic. I must be thinkin' of a postcard I saw or somethin'. Hey, it is kinda flat. Thanks for pointin' that out."

Man: "You guys always this sarcastic?"

Brent: "Nothin' else to do."

Season 1
Episode 2

Tax Man

First aired: **January 29, 2004**

Writers: **Brent Butt and Mark Farrell**

Director: **David Storey**

Guest stars: **Dan Matheson (as himself), Kevin McDonald (as Marvin Drey, the tax man)**

A TAX MAN, not *the* tax man, arrives at Corner Gas to review its business records. His presence has Oscar and Hank cooking up a scheme to humiliate the auditor. Meanwhile, Lacey's new no-free-coffee-refills policy leaves Dog River residents pining for the good old days.

Taxing situation: An official from the Canada Revenue Agency (Kevin McDonald) hangs out with Karen and Lacey at The Ruby.

HOWLER HIGHLIGHT

Local Man Concerned about Mosquito Problem

ON A ROLE

Kevin McDonald (of *Kids in the Hall* fame) had never heard of *Corner Gas* when executive producer Virginia Thompson approached him to appear on the show. Once he read the script and realized how funny it was, he agreed to do a guest appearance. Coincidentally, Brent Butt sometimes did the warm-up act for studio audiences of *The Kids in the Hall*.

REALITY CHECK

Brent Butt's dad, Herb, was the opposite of his onscreen dad, Oscar. Herb was a fun-loving, gentle man who didn't yell at butterflies.

- *Jackass* makes its debut as Oscar's favourite cuss. "It's a swear word that is in the bible," points out Brent Butt.
- The scene where Oscar is in the basement looking for his tax records was the very first one shot for the series. (Scenes are not filmed in the order they appear onscreen. It's TV magic at work!)
- Brent Leroy drinks "beer" on-camera for the first and only time. After that, he sips "rye" (watered-down cola), a nod to Brent Butt's drink of choice.
- Mark Farrell and Brent Butt are nominated for a Gemini Award for the writing in this episode.
- This episode earned an International Emmy Award nomination in the comedy category.

STYLE ON FILE

Hank wears a Sabu T-shirt (from costume designer Brenda Shenher's collection of Ts), named after a one-hit wonder band from Los Angeles.

TOP PROP

First assistant art director Dan Wright is the man responsible for designing editions of the *Howler*. You'll find him in the photo on the front page of the newspaper used in this episode—he's the man standing out in his field.

TRIVIAL LITTLE NOTHING

For her audition for the role of Karen, Tara Spencer-Nairn was asked to do the "Serpico" scene (the one with Davis in the cop car).

TWISTED WORDS

Marvin Drey (the tax man's name) becomes "Muffin tray."

WATCH FOR IT

- David Storey has directed many episodes of *Corner Gas*. And when he has, you can tell without even reading the credits. His signature touch is shooting scenes through inanimate objects—everything from closets to bookshelves, as in this episode. Hence Brent's nickname for him: "Thru Storey." David explains his direction quirk this way: "Because we're shooting comedy and not drama, I can't be moving the camera all the time. This is my way of giving the shots more visual impact."
- While filming the scene where Brent is by the gas pumps talking to the tax man, a prairie storm started to rumble. Although the script called for the scene to continue outdoors, the crew and cast were forced to move into the Corner Gas store to avoid the wind and rain. If you look carefully, you'll see that the store's shelves are nearly empty.

QUIPS AND QUOTES

Tax man: "I just need to speak to your father to verify a few things."

Brent: "I don't think he's here. I think he went to Hawaii."

Tax man: "Hawaii?"

Brent: "Not Hawaii. Somewhere cheaper than that. Red Deer."

•

Emma (after overhearing Oscar yell at someone on the phone): "Who was that?"

Oscar: "I don't know. Some jackass!"

Squeeze play: Brent shows off his talent for pumping gas and daydreaming at the same time.

Season 1
Episode 3

First aired: **February 4, 2004**

Writers: **Mark Farrell and Paul Mather**

Director: **David Storey**

8

Co-op, the everything store of the Prairies, is mentioned for the first time.

Pilates Twist

LACEY IS BAFFLED that the people of Dog River are miffed when she offers "free" Pilates classes. Brent and Hank are two peas in a pod when it comes to their clothes sense, but is the town big enough to handle two dapper dudes? Meanwhile, Oscar ponders his mortality after undertaking a project to build himself a snazzy coffin.

Double trouble: Hank and Brent are perplexed by their shared fashion sense.

POPPED CULTURE

- Wanda says, "Nice going, Gandalf"—a reference to a wizard in *Lord of the Rings*.
- One of many comic book references from Brent: "Buttons are like kryptonite for me"—an allusion to Superman and pieces of his exploded home planet, Krypton.

QUIPS AND QUOTES

Lacey (trying to get Brent to sign up for Pilates classes): "Oh, come on, Brent. Don't you want to unify your mind and body?"

Brent: "I'm not going to put all of my eggs in one basket."

•

Oscar (as he is designing his coffin): "Here, mark my height. I'm going for a custom fit."

Emma: "Don't worry if it's a little tight. We'll stuff you in. Just make sure the saw is sharp."

•

Lacey (referring to Brent and Hank's matching plaid shirts): "Nice blouses, boys."

•

Brent: "*No fear*. You know where I read that?"

Lacey: "Where?"

Brent: "On the T-shirt of a kid working down at the Co-op. He didn't let fear stand in his way. He stood there bravely bagging onions."

REALITY CHECK

Eric Peterson is pretty handy with tools and could likely make both a coffin and a book-shelf. He was a stage carpenter early on in his working life.

TWISTED WORDS

- "Coffin plans" become "coffee plants."
- Brent boasts that his shirt has style, plus comfort, or "stylumfort."

WATCH FOR IT

- The Canadian flags that were by the cash register in the Corner Gas store for the first two episodes have disappeared.
- Prop master Jay Robertson's fingers make an uncredited cameo appearance. You see them briefly as Oscar's coffin/bookshelf falls apart.

Dictionary of Saskatchewanisms, brought to you by Corner Gas

Biffie: toilet or outhouse

Boh: short for Bohemian, a Saskatchewan beer made by Molson Breweries

Bunnyhug: hooded sweatshirt

Butterfly: Women's Fancy Shawl dance, often performed at Aboriginal weddings in Saskatchewan, and symbolizing the butterfly

Calhoun ("cal-hoon"): A very large person (possibly a derivative from professional wrestling legend William "Haystack" Calhoun)

Calved: died, or quit working; as in, "My pickup calved on me."

Coins: testicles

Hoof: walk or kick; almost anything foot related

L.B.S. or L.B.: liquor store

Mountain: a small hill

Mountain range: two small hills

Noodling: thinking

Pil: short for Pilsner, a Saskatchewan beer made by Molson Breweries

Pinned 'er: to travel or leave a scene in a hurry

Rig wig: Saskatchewanian who moved to Alberta, made a lot of money in the oil industry, then returns to Saskatchewan to toss his money around

Slap: close-fisted punch

Slapped snotless: punch repeatedly

Stumpwit: an unintelligent person

Vi-Co: a type of chocolate milk, introduced in western Canada in the mid-1950s

Yabber: a conversation with little value

Season 1
Episode 4

Oh Baby

First aired: **February 11, 2004**
Writers: **Brent Butt and Andrew Carr**
Director: **Henry Sarwer-Foner**

3

Brent attempts to impress Lacey with his babysitting skills. The town is skeptical, since Wanda's six-year-old son, Tanner, has a history of striking terror in his wranglers. While Brent is away from the gas station, Oscar arrives to take over as boss man and trouble follows.

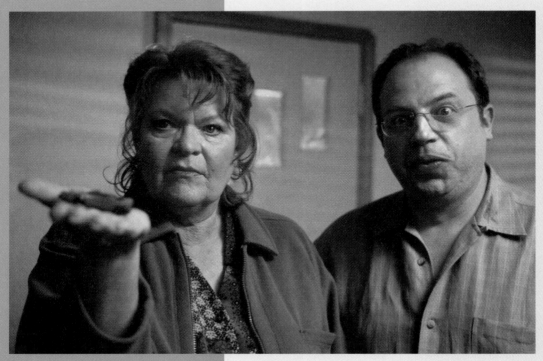

Babysitter 911: Emma saves the day for Brent.

- Viewers are introduced to Wanda's son, Tanner Vincent Dollard.
- We see the inside of Wanda's house, complete with textbooks and oodles of toys strewn everywhere.
- When Emma arrives at Wanda's house to save the day, special effects are used to make Emma appear as if she is surrounded by a ring of mystical glowing light. This is the first ever special-effects shot of the series.

POPPED CULTURE

Brent's babysitting experience is a nod to classic slasher films like *Friday the 13th*, *Halloween*, and *Nightmare on Elm Street*.

REALITY CHECK

When Brent tries to guess Lacey's second name, his guesses are Esther, Charlene, Gerti, Sunshine, and Fern. Gabrielle Miller's middle name is Sunshine. Gerti (Thauberger) is the name of one of the drivers on *Corner Gas*. On the show, Brent's middle name is Herbert (the name of his real-life late father). His real-life one is Leroy, which also happens to be his character's last name. Confused? Join the club.

TOP PROPS

- The toy cars that Tanner throws at Brent's head are made of soft silicone. ("I like to tell people that we injected my head with Novocain," Brent explains.) The thump of the cars hitting Brent and the thunk of them hitting the floor were added as sound effects later. "Thank you for all your cards and letters," says Brent. "I was not injured."
- Don't go looking for the book *Groovy Parents, Smart Kids*, by Dr. Spearmint Fur. It was made up—obvious, if you consider the author's name. But strangely enough, supervising producer Paul Mather co-authored a book titled *How Not to Completely Suck as a New Parent*.
- In a scene filmed at the bar, mayonnaise is squirted onto a hamburger by a twitchy customer. The director wanted "hang time" on the mayo, so the props department concocted a recipe of caulking, glue, and mayo. Ick.

TWISTED WORDS

"Child psychology" morphs into "chives on top of me."

WATCH FOR IT

- The budgie in the birdcage hanging above Hank's head in the flashback sequence doesn't move. It's fake. The birdie sound effects were added in post-production. Endangering an actor with possible falling waste matter from a real bird wasn't an option.
- The names of the show's writers are written on the chalkboard in the scene where bar patrons take bets on the outcome of Brent's babysitting experience.

Hide and seek: Brent and Lacey find themselves under attack while babysitting.

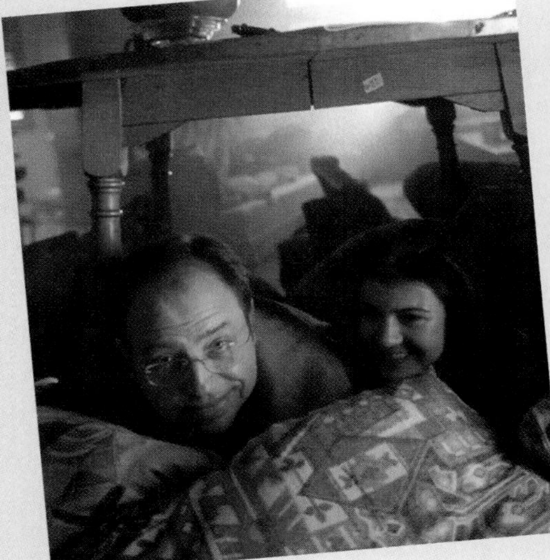

Season 1
Episode 5

First aired: **February 18, 2004**

Writers: **Mark Farrell and Paul Mather**

Director: **Rob King**

Guest star: **Julie Stewart**

6

Grad '68

SOMEONE SPRAY-PAINTED "Grad 68" on Dog River's water tower and Karen is determined to find the culprit—but finding helpful witnesses may mean this cold case stays chilled. Meanwhile, Brent causes confusion with new bathroom signs at the gas station. Lacey's hopes of becoming a columnist for the *Howler* are dashed. Her rejection by the newspaper that claims to take stories from anyone has her determined to prove she has the "write" stuff.

Stoop and snoop: Karen enlists the help of an expert (Julie Stewart) to solve the grad '68 mystery.

But seriously: Karen takes her duties to heart as an officer of the law.

OOPS

Davis comes out of the bathroom, saying that it smells great. In Season 2's Smell of Freedom, it's revealed that Davis lost his sense of smell as a child.

REALITY CHECK

At first, the character of Wanda was going to be more of a hoser type, but writer Mark Farrell said, "Let's go in the opposite direction. Let's make her a genius."

TWISTED WORDS

Oscar turns "mullet" into "mull head."

HOWLER HIGHLIGHTS

- Grad '68 Solved
- Give a Hoot, Stamp Out Graffiti

ON A ROLE

Julie Stewart from *Cold Squad* appears as a paint-store clerk and says, "Cold case? Who cares?"

COINCIDENTALLY

Fred Ewanuick, Nancy Robertson, and Tara Spencer-Nairn have all appeared as guest stars on the TV series *Cold Squad*.

QUIPS AND QUOTES

Davis (angrily): "At least I'm not ..."

Karen: "Blonde? Pretty? Thin?"

Davis (with a pout): "*I'm* pretty ..."

Mayor Fitzgerald (Cavan Cunningham) appears on the show for the first time.

Season 1
Episode 6

First aired: **February 25, 2004**

Writer: **Brent Butt**

Director: **David Storey**

World's Biggest Thing

IN HOPES OF luring tourists to Dog River, a plan is hatched to build the world's biggest something. But what? Other Prairie towns have a giant egg, or a moose, or a magpie. The mayor's grandmother suggests a hoe, which causes a rash of racey jokes. Meanwhile, Oscar tries to fend off the advances of Lacey, whom he believes is out to ruin his marriage.

Buzz worthy: Tisdale, Saskatchewan, Brent Butt's hometown, lays claim to the world's largest honeybee.

The creation of the hoe in post-production is one of the first large-scale special effects of the series.

POPPED CULTURE

At the beginning of the episode, a chalkboard behind the cash in the Corner Gas store lists the names Peter Parker of *Spider-Man*; Marge Simpson of *The Simpsons*; Jean-Luc Picard of *Star Trek: The Next Generation*; and Arthur Fonzarelli of *Happy Days*.

TRIVIAL LITTLE NOTHING

"Wullerton" is mentioned in the *Star Wars* film series: It's the capital city of the planet Draenell's Point. Although Brent Butt insists this is just a coincidence. "I picked Wullerton 'cause it sounded like a town I could hate," he says.

Big Things Found in Saskatchewan

Combine in the sky, in Allan

Lesia the Ukrainian girl, in Canora

Canadian dollar coin, in Churchbridge

Tomahawk, in Cut Knife

Coffee pot and cup, in Davidson

Hockey cards, in Kelvington

Wally the woolly mammoth, in Kyle

Mac the moose, in Moose Jaw

Giant ice cube melt, in North Battleford

Pitchfork, in Regina

Baseball cap, in Rocanville

Honeybee, in Tisdale

Grasshopper, in Wilkie

REALITY CHECK

- The Dog River–Wullerton rivalry is based on the real-life one between Brent Butt's hometown of Tisdale, Saskatchewan, and nearby Melfort, which has a bigger population. According to Brent, "Every town has their own Wullerton. I wanted to play that up—that pointless hatred for no reason."
- As the creative team brainstormed on the world's biggest something for the script, Brent came up with hoe. He knew he was on to something when Mark Farrell and David Storey cracked up.

QUIPS AND QUOTES

Oscar: "I didn't know whether to tell you this or not, but someone in town has a crush on me."

Emma: "A crush ... on you? You couldn't get a dog to lick you if you were covered in gravy."

Oscar: "What the hell are you talking about? Dogs lick me all the time."

Emma: "So who's got a crush on you? Is Helen Keller back in town?"

TOP PROPS

- Although many people come to Rouleau, Saskatchewan, to look for the world's biggest hoe, they won't find it. The only part of the hoe that physically existed was the handle. The rest of it was created through computer graphics in post-production.
- On *Corner Gas*, Brent drives a yellow, two-door 1968 Oldsmobile Cutlass. He had six cars to choose from for his character. He chose the Cutlass because it reminded him of his favourite car, the 1975 Dodge Dart Sport that he booted around in as a teenager.
- The cinder block that Emma hurls at a skunk is made of Styrofoam. She managed to hit director of photography Ken Krawczyk with it twice. What an arm!

Season 1

Episode 7

First aired: **March 3, 2004**
Writer: **Mark Farrell**
Director: **Henry Sarwer-Foner**
Guest stars: **Peter Oldring (as Stephen), Mark Dieter (as Paul Kinistino)**

1

6

All My Ex's

THE PEOPLE of Dog River play defence in order to protect Lacey from her ex-fiancé, who has come from Toronto to pay her a visit. Meanwhile, Emma gets tough with her doctor-phobic husband; Karen shows off her billy stick, named Jennifer; and the new police interrogation room becomes the town hot spot.

REALITY CHECK

In the fantasy sequence, Brent and Lacey seductively eat a chili cheese dog together. Truth is, Gabrielle Miller, who plays Lacey, is a vegetarian. The props department made the chili out of veggie ground round for her.

Under investigation: Davis treats Lacey's visiting ex, Stephen (guest star Peter Oldring), with suspicion.

TOP PROP

Karen wouldn't catch any speeders with this radar gun. It was constructed from parts of a box-style flashlight, a mirror, and an LED display.

TRIVIAL LITTLE NOTHING

Filming has to be scheduled carefully around the times when Officer Karen Pelly wears her police hat. The weight of it leaves a big crease across her forehead that takes an hour to disappear. Whoever said police work was a cakewalk?

QUIPS AND QUOTES

Emma: "You're going to the doctor."

Oscar: "Over my dead body!"

Emma: "Well, that would speed up the process."

•

Paul the barman (asking Brent about going to the doctor): "Did he give you one of those ...?"

Brent: "Oh, yeah. He put the 'pro' in prostate."

Paul: "Well, it's gotta be done."

Brent: "I guess. I wish he wasn't so enthusiastic about it though, ya know? The guy went at me like he was trying to get the last pickle out of the jar."

•

Brent: "You're going to be around for a long time."

Oscar: "How do you know?"

Brent: "I've angered the karma gods and this is my punishment."

In Praise of Chili Cheese Dogs

Brent has described chili cheese dogs as "nature's most perfect food." As a stand-up comic, he performed frequently at Toronto's Laugh Resort and would pick up a snack from a (now gone) restaurant below the comedy club. "No kidding, I'd eat six chili cheese dogs in a week," says Brent. "Now I work them into *Corner Gas* scripts any chance I get. Jay Robertson, our props master, makes the best chili I've ever tasted." Don't take Brent's word for it: Whip up a batch yourself. This recipe comes courtesy of Jay, who grew up on the chili his dad made.

W.J. Robbie Robertson's Chili

1 pound (0.5 kg) extra-lean ground meat

1 large white onion, diced

1 14 oz (398 mL) can condensed tomato soup

1 19 oz (540 mL) can red kidney beans

1 green pepper, diced

2 cups (500 mL) sliced fresh mushrooms

1/4 cup (50 mL) chili powder

1 tsp (5 mL) brown sugar

1 generous squirt of ketchup

salt and pepper to taste

shredded cheddar cheese as garnish

- In a large skillet over medium-high heat, brown meat. Drain excess fat. Add remaining ingredients and simmer for at least one hour.
- Serve straight up, or spoon chili over a hot dog and top with shredded cheddar cheese. Belch heartily.

Director Henry Sarwer-Foner is nominated for a Canadian Comedy Award for this episode.

Season 1
Episode 8

First aired: **March 10, 2004**
Writer: **Chris Finn**
Director: **Rob King**
Guest stars: **Mike Wilmot (as Cousin Carl), Dale Wilson (as the Man from Glad)**

Cousin Carl

Everyone in Dog River but Brent seems to like his successful cousin Carl, who is visiting from England, where he now works. The town's talent show proves to Brent that his seemingly perfect relative is perfectly imperfect. Meanwhile, Davis's love of puppetry takes a bad turn post-talent night, and Oscar nets a bit of cash from his old stubbie beer bottles.

2

9

All in the family: Trouble's brewing for Brent when his cousin Carl (Mike Wilmot) comes to town.

Rob W. King is nominated for a Gemini Award for Best Direction in a Comedy Program or Series for this episode.

Happy face: The man from Glad (Dale Wilson) appears in Brent's dream sequence.

POPPED CULTURE

Lacey mentions *The Gong Show*, the original reality talent show from the mid-1970s, hosted by Chuck Barris.

COINCIDENTALLY

Guest star Mike Wilmot (as Cousin Carl) is a stand-up comic who has been very successful in England. He is a long-time buddy of Brent's. The two played the comedy club circuit together and happened to be on a month-long tour together at the same time that Brent was developing *Corner Gas*. Brent said to Mike, "If this thing goes, you should come and do an episode. You can play my cousin or something." A year later, Mike's agent in England said to him, "There's a script here for a show in Canada. They want you to be in it." Mike picked up the script and saw it was for a comedy called *Corner Gas*. When he read the episode name, Cousin Carl, Mike was shocked. "I thought this was just drunken bar talk," he said to his agent.

QUIPS AND QUOTES

Brent (after tasting his dad's homemade beer, Oscarbrau): "Honest to God, Dad, it tastes like you beat a skunk to death with a salmon!"

•

Mrs. Jensen: "When your father ran the place, the customer was always respected."

Oscar (to Brent): "Hey, jackass, stop talking to this old wing nut and pump my gas!"

Brent: "Well, he's a people person."

•

Angels (in Brent's dream sequence): "Your pudding bath is ready."

Brent: "Is this my happy place?"

REALITY CHECK

The insurance store in Dog River that also sells liquor is based on a real business in Rouleau, Saskatchewan, run by the town's mayor. The writers of *Corner Gas* loved the concept of the one-stop shop so much that they worked it into a number of scripts.

Mad about plaid: Brent dresses up for the local talent show.

STYLE ON FILE

Although many wardrobe pieces are shared between real Brent and TV Brent, the plaid jacket that he wears for the Dog River talent show is not one of them. It was a rental.

TOP PROP

Where do you find a case of stubbies these days? Props master Jay Robertson hunted down a couple of cases of Heidelberg beer bottles at a Regina antique store.

Season 1
Episode 9

First aired: **March 17, 2004**

Writer: **Paul Mather**

Director: **Robert de Lint**

4

4

Cell Phone

IT'S A SMALL WORLD after all when Brent gets a new cell phone and Davis is keen to better him with his own technological toys. Lacey tries to schmooze her way into Dog River's exclusive chamber of commerce. The demolition of a historic landmark might be exactly the cause she needs to become the organization's newest member. Oscar has his own obsession—trying to win stuffed toys from a new game at the Dog River Hotel in which a giant claw is manoeuvred to grab prizes.

An office and a gentleman: Davis gets down to police business.

QUIPS AND QUOTES

Brent (on his cell phone): "No, Dad, I didn't lose it ... well, how could I be talkin' to you on it if I lost it?"

•

Oscar: "Hey, jackass. Where is the shuffle-board table?"

Paul the barman: "It's gone."

Oscar: "Did it grow legs and walk out of the bar?"

Paul: "It got kicked out because it called me a jackass."

Fred Ewanuick receives a nomination for a Leo Award, Music, Comedy, or Variety Program or Series: Best Performance or Host, for this episode.

HOWLER HIGHLIGHT

Chamber of Commerce Announces New Members and Almost Everyone Gets In

TOP PROP

Brent's teeny-weeny cell phone was made from a flip-open magnifying glass and buttons from a toy cell phone.

Leisure pursuit: Hank has perfected the art of hanging out.

Season 1

Episode 10

First aired: **March 24, 2004**

Writers: **Brent Butt, Mark Farrell, and Paul Mather**

Director: **Mark Farrell**

Guest stars: **Peter Kelamis (as Bob Lang), Colin Mochrie (as himself)**

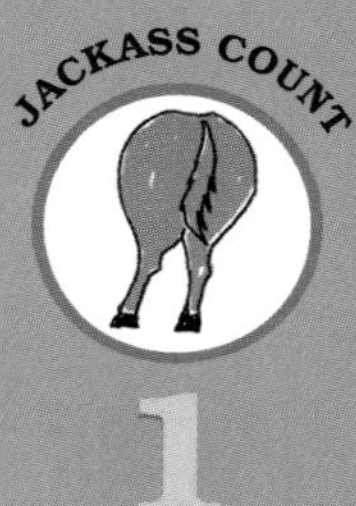

1

10

Comedy Night

AN OUT-OF-TOWN COMEDIAN in town to perform at Dog River's comedy night has Brent in a huff. Hank, however, is star-struck by the comic and worms his way into being the MC for the event. Hank tries to hone his comedy act and his handling of hecklers with a little help from Lacey, which he takes too far. While the town is busy with comic antics, the women's book club turns a new page by welcoming Brent.

Mug shots: Oscar and Brent are in search of a caffeine fix at The Ruby.

POPPED CULTURE

When asked how he is enjoying the book he's reading—*The Life of Pi*, by Yann Martel—Brent responds by doing his best Tony the Tiger imitation: "The tiger book? It's GRRRRR-EAT!"

Writer and supervising producer Mark Farrell slips into the director's chair for the first time.

REALITY CHECK

Many of the show's writers have done stand-up comedy and improv. All the heckler lines used are phrases that comedians know all too well.

WATCH FOR IT

The book shown at the end of the episode, *Dingoes in Their Natural Habitat*, is credited to "author" Jay Robertson (*Corner Gas*'s props master). It's a fictional title, created by the props team as a little joke on their leader.

ON A ROLE

- Colin Mochrie was one of Mark Farrell's favourite guest stars: "It was great because Colin was willing to make fun of himself. I like it when guest stars aren't unveiled before an episode. I like the idea of viewers sitting there, watching and minding their own business, and being jolted out of their seats." Surprise!
- Comedian Peter Kelamis is another old pal of Brent's. Although Brent kindly invites his buddies to be guest stars, they always play jerks—Cousin Carl, Bob Lang, Rocket Ronnie Raymore. The reason for this phenomenon? "I'm trying to make Canada hate my friends. It's fun for me," explains Brent.

STYLE ON FILE

The Trooper T-shirt that Hank wears in the cold opener (the very beginning of the episode that opens the show, even before the theme song plays and the credits roll), when he's in The Ruby talking to Brent, is the same one he wears during the opening credits. Trooper was one of Canada's most rockin' bands in the 1980s.

HOWLER HIGHLIGHT

New Call Centre to Be Built in Wullerton

QUIPS AND QUOTES

Lacey: "Karen, I'm glad you're here. Look, we need to talk about the book club."

Karen: "I thought the first rule of book club was, you don't talk about book club."

Lacey: "That's fight club."

Karen: "How do you know about fight club?"

•

Brent: "I love books. I'm a voluptuous reader."

TOP PROPS

- The beers in the bar aren't the real deal. De-alcoholized beer, including Molson Excel, is used. Brent's rye is watered-down cola.
- Finding multiple copies of *The Saint of New York*, by Leslie Charteris, for the book club scenes proved to be a challenge for the props department. It sourced copies from all over North America, including one edition from Florida.

What's in store: Brent and Wanda demonstrate plenty of counter intelligence.

Season 1
Episode 11

First aired: **March 21, 2004**

Writers: **Brent Butt and Andrew Carr**

Director: **Robert de Lint**

Guest stars: **Pamela Wallin, Farley Flex, Jake Gold, Sass Jordan, Zack Werner (as themselves)**

7

Hook, Line and Sinker

BRENT PUTS UP A SIGN to boost business at the gas station and The Ruby, but his attempts at catchy phrases for it has caused a battle of words between him and Lacey. Meanwhile, Brent and Emma start thinking that Oscar might be losing his memory when his can of pasta keeps going AWOL, and Karen sees a sensual side of Hank on a fishing trip.

Slogans That Appeared on the Corner Gas and Ruby Sign

- While waiting for slow service at Corner Gas, enjoy a meal at The Ruby.
- The food at The Ruby sucks.
- Brent is an ass.
- If you think our bathrooms are dirty, you should see our kitchen.
- Karen slept with Hank.

Hook up: Karen discovers a sensual side to Hank while fishing.

ON A ROLE

The job of executive producer is an all-encompassing one—just ask Virginia Thompson. She went on an errand for Pamela Wallin (born in Wadena, Saskatchewan, by the way) to get hair rollers, then met Pamela and led her, by car, to the Rouleau set. On the way, Pamela, driving in her own car, passed the executive producer when Montreal-born Virginia slowed to look at the canola fields in bloom. As Wallin zoomed past her, confident that she could get to Rouleau on her own, Virginia thought, "Oh my God! I've lost our guest star."

STYLE ON FILE

Hank trades in his signature baseball cap for a fishing hat.

POPPED CULTURE

Hank fantasizes about Darth Vader from *Star Wars* fighting Spock from *Star Trek*.

OOPS

In the scene where Emma and Oscar are talking to Brent and Wanda at the counter in the Corner Gas store, a can of pasta is sitting on a shelf behind Oscar. In the next shot, the can has vanished.

REALITY CHECK

- Brent Butt likes to sing but admits that he's "terrible." That didn't stop him from forming a band in high school called Fast Exit and playing gigs.
- The setting for a romantic fishing scene between Karen and Hank could not have been more uncomfortable for the crew and actors involved. It was filmed near a river in the Qu'Appelle Valley, and "it was really, really hot, about 35 degrees Celsius," remembers Tara. "We were down by the water and there were bugs flying into our mouths. It was almost impossible to get through the scenes. We felt disgusting, soaking with sweat. It was pretty gross, but the scenes turned out so amazing."
- The "real" Hank is featured throughout *this* episode, but did you know that his stand-in is seen on every episode? Say what?! It's true. In the opening credits, there is a wide shot, in which the camera pans from a waving Brent to Lacey watering flowers. In between, for a split second, you can see Hank leaning over the engine of his truck, the hood up. But it's not Fred Ewanuick. It's actually lead props guy Roger Roscoe dressed in Hank garb.

Who's the boss: Brent Butt looks every inch a Saskatchewan movie mogul.

TWISTED WORDS

Wanda shows off her ability to rearrange letters to make a new sentence. The slogan "Come for the oil change. Stay for the grease" became "Choose Glenn Frey for a ménage à trois."

QUIPS AND QUOTES

Brent (singing in front of the *Canadian Idol* judges): "It would never rain in Dog River if I could squeegee the sky ..." (That line of improvised lyrics was something Brent came up with "in about four seconds.")

•

Karen (to Hank): "Kiss me, fish man."

•

Brent: "Hey, is *poop face* hyphenated?"

Season 1
Episode 12

First aired: **April 21, 2004**

Writers: **Mark Farrell, Iain MacLean, and Paul Mather**

Director: **David Storey**

Guest stars: **TSN's Jennifer Frances Hedger (as herself), TSN's Darren Dutchyshen (as himself), Jamie Hutchinson (as Rocket Ronnie Raymore)**

7

Face Off

IT'S HOCKEY SEASON in Dog River, and the team is pitted against a rival team from Stonewood for its first game. Brent's prowess as a goalie seems to be ignored by his teammates, so he begins to entertain offers from the competition. Although in need of some good coaching, the team is reluctant to take advice from Lacey, an unlikely hockey expert. Oscar and Emma have trouble making it from the car to the rink, courtesy of another Oscar screw-up.

Net worth: Brent gets a taste of superstardom as goalie.

- This episode earns a Gemini Award nomination for a Best Ensemble Performance in a Comedy Program or Series.
- Brent Butt and Andrew Carr win a Leo Award, Music, Comedy, or Variety Program or Series—Best Screenwriting for this episode.
- Gabrielle Miller's performance as coach of the Dog River River Dogs wins her a Leo Award.

QUIPS AND QUOTES

Ronnie: "Celebrating a bit much for a tie, aren't we, boys?"

Davis: "You're just mad because you didn't beat us."

Hank: "Yeah, you poor tie-ers!"

Brent: "Sleep well knowing you don't suck any less than we do!"

•

Wanda's hockey talk:

"Bender in the beer hole" means *elbow in the mouth*

"Premature" means *offside*

"Twine tickler" means *goal*

HOWLER HIGHLIGHT

River Dogs Almost Win!

ON A ROLE

Hockey player Brian Hlushko plays young Brent in a flashback scene.

COINCIDENTALLY

Brent Butt and guest star Jamie Hutchinson served as each other's best man at their weddings.

Saskatchewan at Centre Ice

It's amazing but true: Saskatchewan produces more NHLers than any other province in the country. Here are some of the goal-setting players born in Saskatchewan:

- The legendary Gordie Howe, born in Floral
- Goalie Glenn Hall, born in Humboldt
- Max Bentley, known as the Dipsy Doodle Dandy from Delisle
- Gerry James, born in Regina, who made history by playing in both the CFL's Grey Cup (with the Winnipeg Blue Bombers) and the NHL's Stanley Cup (with the Toronto Maple Leafs) finals in the same year
- Bryan Trottier, from Val Marie, a member of six Stanley Cup winning teams (four with the New York Islanders and two with the Pittsburgh Penguins)
- Hayley Wickenheiser, described as the world's best female hockey player, born in Shaunavon.

REALITY CHECK

- Brent Butt's hockey position of choice is goalie, and so is Fred Ewanuick's. For this episode, Fred played forward instead.
- Neither Nancy Robertson nor Gabrielle Miller follow hockey, but they really worked at being able to use hockey lingo and sound convincing.
- The word *jackass* has been a favourite of Brent Butt's for a long time. It is also a word he connects to his long-time pal and fellow comic Jamie Hutchinson, who guest stars in this episode. Brent set up his phone to respond to a verbal command of "jackass" by dialing Jamie's number. And yes, they have remained good friends.

Season 1
Episode 13

First aired: **April 28, 2004**

Writers: **Brent Butt, Mark Farrell, and Paul Mather**

Director: **David Storey**

I Love Lacey

FUNNY THINGS HAPPEN on the way to the Grey Cup in Regina as the gang from Dog River show their football spirit. A visit to Oscar's crazy old buddy turns out to be a dead-end for Hank and Oscar. Brent runs out of gas en route to the game but discovers that there's a spark when it comes to his relationship with Lacey. Emma and Wanda engage in retail therapy at their favourite store and find more than they bargained for.

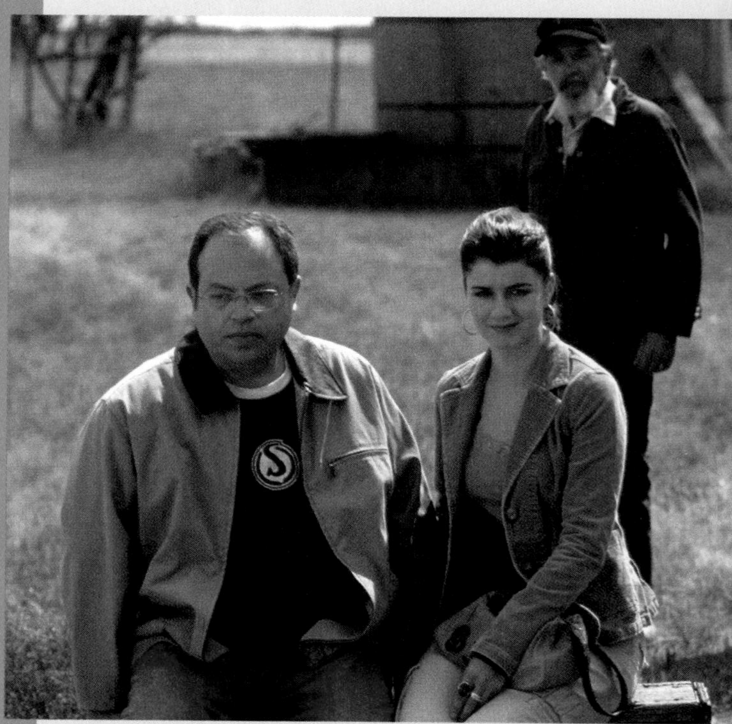

Running on empty: Brent and Lacey's trip to the Grey Cup goes awry when Brent's car runs out of gas.

QUIPS AND QUOTES

Karen: "Isn't it weird for you to go to a scalper?"

Davis: "Why? Because I'm a Cree man? I resent that."

Karen: "Because you're a police officer and scalping tickets is illegal."

•

Brent (to Lacey): "Physical activity and direct sunlight are two of my favourite things. If you were playing the bagpipes, this would be a perfect day."

- David Storey's direction of this episode wins him a Leo Award, Music, Comedy, or Variety Program or Series.
- Brenda Shenher receives a Gemini Award nomination for Best Costume Design, for this episode.

REALITY CHECK

Many fans have wondered why everyone isn't bundled up in winter clothing for the Grey Cup in this episode. The scene was actually filmed in August, during a hot spell, and the actors were already practically melting in their warmer clothes.

WATCH FOR IT

Director David Storey is at it again. He uses his signature shot—from the perspective of inanimate objects—once more in this episode. Brent is filmed from the open trunk of a car.

Playing the Field in Regina

Portions of I Love Lacey were filmed around Taylor Field, home to the Saskatchewan Roughriders. The man for whom the stadium was named was Neil "Piffles" Taylor, an agile football and rugby player known for his near-psychic ability to figure out his opponents' strategies. Taylor's sporting career was interrupted when he joined the Royal Flying Corps during World War I. His plane was shot down over France, and he became a prisoner of war. After the war was over, he returned home and resumed playing football, despite that he had only one eye because of a war injury. It's been reported that a match between Calgary and Regina had to be stopped mid-game so that Taylor could find his glass eye: It had popped out during a fierce tackle. Upon his death in 1946, the stadium was named Taylor Field in his memory.

Season 2
Episode 1

First aired: **October 5, 2004**
Writers: **Brent Butt and Mark Farrell**
Director: **David Storey**

The Brent Effect

10

Hawkin's Cheezies (the snack food of choice for many Saskatchewanians) make an appearance on the store shelves of the gas station.

AFTER A NEAR KISS on Grey Cup day, Brent and Lacey ponder what it means to their relationship, if anything. Meanwhile, Karen shows off her investigative skills when gunshots around Dog River are reported and all roads lead to Davis. Oscar is in big trouble after he spends the money Emma was saving for a new blender on an old outboard motor.

Batter up: Oscar upsets Emma when his outboard motor doubles as a mixer.

- To promote the arrival of another season of *Corner Gas*, cast members pump over $70,000 worth of free gas in cities across Canada.
- The debut episode for Season 2 is a ratings winner, with more than 1.5 million viewers.
- Gabrielle Miller wins a Leo Award for her performance in this episode.

QUIPS AND QUOTES

Emma: "Is that why you need the money? For a stupid outboard motor?"

Oscar: "None of your business. Maybe I'm buying you a present."

Emma: "You bought me a plastic butter dish fifteen years ago, and now another present?"

Oscar: "Well, keep it up ... You won't get nothin'!"

•

Wanda (to Lacey): "You almost kissed [Brent]? Wow. That's a big deal ... for grade seven!"

•

Karen: "I know you're my senior officer, so I say this with all due respect: How stupid are you!? You can't just fire your gun off willy-nilly."

Davis: "It wasn't willy-nilly. It was at crows."

REALITY CHECK

- Fred Ewanuick downs copious amounts of root beer in an effort to create the perfect belch for a scene where Hank lets one rip in front of his buddies near the Dog River Hotel. It didn't quite work, so the sound of a full-scale belch was added in post-production.
- Before show biz called, Gabrielle Miller worked as a waitress and hostess. "I pour a mean cup of coffee," she says.

WATCH FOR IT

- Director David Storey likes to have things like farm machinery in the background of scenes, but one particular writer does not, believing it detracts from the comedy. As a playful act of revenge, David placed a man wearing a cowboy hat on a horse in the background of a scene where Lacey and Emma are walking outside the post office, talking about Brent. "You can see the horse clearly at the top of the scene," explains David. "I put that in there to get back at that writer."
- This time, David Storey shoots through the (backless) fridge at the store and through (backless) cupboards as well.
- Stop the press! The Ruby now has new curtains.

TRIVIAL LITTLE NOTHING

It was Brent's idea to make his TV alter-ego the best looking guy in town.

POPPED CULTURE

Wanda tells Hank, "You're a regular Jay Lame-o,"—a nod to *The Tonight Show* host, Jay Leno.

Well read: Brent and Hank choose comic books as their prime source of entertainment.

Season 2
Episode 2

First aired: **October 12, 2004**

Writers: **Mark Farrell and Paul Mather**

Director: **Robert de Lint**

Guest star: **Darryl Sittler (as himself)**

15

Wedding Card

SCANDAL HITS the Leroy family when Brent discovers that his parents were never married. Davis launches into wedding planner mode and proceeds to put together a lavish wedding ceremony. Lacey has a cause of her own. She's out to help Oscar learn to read, an inability he's not aware he even has. Meanwhile, Brent and Hank are at odds with one another when a childhood dispute over the ownership of a Darryl Sittler rookie card rears its head yet again.

Star-struck: Hockey legend Darryl Sittler visits Dog River.

OOPS

We see a photo of Oscar and Emma, each dressed up in a white jumpsuit and wig to look like Elvis, from their wedding in 1965. However, Elvis didn't wear those jumpsuits until the early 1970s.

Wedding belles: Emma and Oscar entertain guests Brent and Lacey at their reception.

HOWLER HIGHLIGHTS

- Local Man Concerned about Mosquito Problem (this edition of the *Howler* is used whenever a character has a copy of the paper but the paper is not specific to the episode's action or storyline)
- New Bylaw Proposed

ON A ROLE

The cast and crew of *Corner Gas* don't become star-struck very often, but they were with Darryl Sittler on set. CTV exec Brent Haynes was there and had the thrill of a lifetime talking hockey with the legendary player. Too shy to ask for autographs from their hero, some of the crew asked costume designer Brenda Shenher to make the request for them.

QUIPS AND QUOTES

Wanda (upon learning that Brent's parents weren't really married): "You're actually a bastard."

Brent: "I prefer the term *love child*."

•

Oscar (about his upcoming nuptials): "Daisy arch? You'll never get me under one of those death traps."

COINCIDENTALLY

- In this episode, we learn that Oscar and Emma have been together for 35 years. Eric Peterson and Janet Wright have been friends for the same length of time.
- Hank, upon seeing The Ruby decorated for the wedding reception, says, "They've turned it into a gay bar." In Ruby Reborn, Season 1, Hank says the same thing when Lacey redecorates.

REALITY CHECK

Nancy Robertson (Wanda) may be small, but she is mighty. During the scene where she dances with the male stripper, then pushes him out the door, she shoved him so hard that he went flying and nearly landed on his very toned bottom. "I felt bad," says Nancy.

Boogie fever: Wanda busts a move at Emma's bachelorette party.

Season 2
Episode 3

First aired: **October 18, 2004**
Writers: **Paul Mather and Kevin White**
Director: **Robert de Lint**

Smell of Freedom

IT'S A BRAVE NEW WORLD for Davis, who regains his sense of smell after a freak accident, but he finds that his partner is nothing to sniff at. Meanwhile, reigning word-game champ Lacey takes on Hank in a spirited showdown, and Brent learns that he has much to learn about his fellow Dog Riverites.

1

16

Game on: Hank and Lacey go head to head in a battle of words.

QUIPS AND QUOTES

Oscar: "You're not going to learn anything from a stupid book."
Brent: "Wise words, Dad."

•

Oscar: "How'd you lose your smell in the first place?"
Davis: "I got hit in the face with a ball."
Oscar: "Then what you need to do is get hit with a ball again."
Davis: "I don't think that'll work."
Oscar: "Why not?"
Davis: "This isn't *Gilligan's Island*."

Running scared: Davis would rather jog than ride with his partner Karen.

OOPS

In Season 1's Grad '68 episode, Davis comments on the bathroom smelling nice. An oops? Writer Paul Mather's explanation is that Davis was just trying to fit in.

STYLE ON FILE

Costume designer Brenda Shenher found the unusual T-shirt Hank wears in this episode—the one with multiple faces and French phrases—in Value Village, a used-clothing store.

TOP PROP

The Neil Diamond album came from the collection of art director Dan Wright.

REALITY CHECK

- As a kid, Brent Butt was the proud owner of the game KerPlunk, featured in this episode.
- Oscar may not like cats, but Eric Peterson does. In fact, he has had cats, dogs, rabbits, and rats as pets.
- Karen is behind the wheel of the police car in this episode—something not seen often. It's not that she's not a good driver, it's just that the car is huge. In order for the cameras to film her clearly, she has to sit on a big pile of padding, to raise her head above the dash. Lorne Cardinal (Davis) is a tall man and doesn't have this problem.

Season 2
Episode 4

First aired: **October 25, 2004**

Writers: **Brent Butt and Mark Farrell**

Director: **David Storey**

Guest star: **Regina mayor Pat Fiacco (as Stan)**

2

7

Whata-phobia

LACEY'S HOPES for a happy birthday are ruined by her fear of balloons. It seems everyone in Dog River has something they are afraid of—except Wanda—and Hank and Brent set out to discover what might strike fear in her. Oscar hooks up with Karen on the sly in an effort to fool Emma into thinking he's a skilled cook.

Scared silly: Lacey tackles her fear of balloons.

Fear factor: Wide-open spaces scare Wanda.

REALITY CHECK

- Karen might be a whiz in the kitchen, but Tara Spencer-Nairn isn't. She's a straight-out-of-the-can, fresh-from-the-box kind of cook.
- Every phobia that Wanda doesn't have, Nancy Robertson does, including claustrophobia. While filming the scene where she's inside the chest, Roger Roscoe, lead props, was off-camera whispering to her that he'd open the lid any time she needed him to. It was Nancy's idea to have some dessert in there with her, a bit of sweet comfort.
- In the scene with balloons in the Corner Gas store at the end of the episode, Gabrielle Miller (Lacey) turned around just before the camera was set to roll, holding a balloon with "Stinky Storey" written on it in marker. It was a little joke played on director and executive producer David Storey.

ON A ROLE

Regina mayor Pat Fiacco makes his world acting debut, as Stan, the owner of the mini-putt golf course. You can see him crack a slight smile when Oscar yells at him.

TOP PROPS

- The spider brought into Corner Gas in an attempt to frighten Wanda was the real thing—a Chilean rose tarantula. First assistant director Pam Wintringham's hand is the one we see in the jar with the spider. A fake spider, created out of a plastic grape, was painted to look like the living, breathing one and used for other shots with Wanda. Post-filming, Carolyn Harris from the set department adopted the tarantula, naming her Rosie.
- Brent Butt's favourite prop is a deck of cards, seen in this episode. He is an avid poker player and likes to practice his shuffling in between takes.

QUIPS AND QUOTES

Oscar (to Emma, after telling her that he is building his own mini-putt course after being banned from Dog River's): "This is not about revenge. This is about getting even."

•

Hank: "I've got something in this box that is going to terrify you."

Wanda: "DNA proof that we are related?"

•

Emma: "He was being a jackass!"

Oscar: "Emma, Emma, Emma. Anger is not the answer."

Brent: "Pot, this is kettle. Kettle, this is pot."

Creep show: Meet the newest cast member, Rosie the tarantula.

Season 2
Episode 5

First aired: **November 2, 2004**
Writers: **Paul Mather and Kevin White**
Director: **Robert de Lint**

Lost and Found

HANK AND BRENT engage in a war of favours. Hank needs help from Brent but won't ask for it. Brent is happy with the status quo—no one owes anyone any favours and he is determined to make sure it stays that way. Meanwhile, Karen is irritating everyone when she takes up playing with a Hacky Sack footbag, and Oscar turns into a treasure hunter when he discovers a perfectly good pair of pants in the ditch.

1

7

Jean scene: Oscar models his roadside find.

QUIPS AND QUOTES

Brent (asking about a singer Wanda and Lacey are going to see perform): "Who's Sarah Harden?"

Lacey: "Oh, she's new."

Wanda: "You're not up on it, or you're not into it?"

Brent: "I might be into it if I was up on it. But I'm not up on it, so I'm not into it. What I'm into, I'm up on."

Lacey: "I'm mostly into what I'm up on, but even though I'm not up on the new stuff, I'm sort of into it."

Wanda: "Prepositions are fun, aren't they?"

•

Davis (to Brent as he looks at the gas station's fully stocked candy display unit): "Nice rack!"

•

Wanda: "You're getting more like [Oscar] every day."

Brent: "Don't be a jackass."

HOWLER HIGHLIGHT

Annual Farm Machinery Expo Huge Success

POPPED CULTURE

Davis makes reference to his hero, Lennie from the TV show *Law & Order*.

REALITY CHECK

- Brent Butt hurt his back while moving the candy display rack into the Corner Gas store. He flew to Vancouver to see his chiropractor for treatment.
- In most scenes, Roger Roscoe, lead props, lay on the ground and threw two footbags in the air while Tara Spencer-Nairn timed her leg movements to his tosses so it would appear she was kicking them up. However, in a scene filmed in the store, Tara successfully did it all on her own—*and* on the first take.
- Karen's irritation over someone stealing her footbag was inspired by a real-life incident involving Mark Farrell and his volleyball. He became agitated when he thought one of his writing colleagues took it. "He made our life a living hell," said one co-worker. This storyline pokes fun at Mark and his unnatural attachment to his volleyball.
- The idea for the owing favours storyline came from writer Kevin White, who needed his neighbour's help to move something heavy but wouldn't ask him because it would mean having to help his neighbour in turn with building a fence.

TRIVIAL LITTLE NOTHING

The name Hacky Sack is copyrighted. Permission to use the word had to be obtained before filming. The generic name for the bean bag is footbag.

Feet first: Karen kicks it up a notch with her footbag.

Season 2
Episode 6

First aired: **November 9, 2004**

Writers: **Mark Farrell and Paul Mather**

Director: **David Storey**

Guest star: **Lloyd Robertson (as himself)**

2

17

Brent watches a Saskatchewan Roughriders' football game on his new television.

Poor Brent

Brent grows up by making an adult investment in a big-screen television, then inexplicably finds himself the object of pity among his friends. Wanda leaps into the handmade jewellery business and wins Lacey as a customer, but at what price? Oscar's criticism of Emma for never putting the lid back on the sugar bowl leads to a battle of the most trifling kind.

Meet Buck Naked: Oscar goes *au naturel* for the ladies.

Token of love: Oscar worms his way into Emma's good books with an amethyst bracelet.

Viewers see inside Brent's house for the first time.

POPPED CULTURE

Brent wonders whether his new TV might be too big, since he has Burt Reynolds burned onto his retina, and he tells Wanda that he watched *Cannonball Run—Director's Cut*.

OOPS

The case of the mysterious changing numbers: In the scene where Lacey is talking about the price of french fries to Wanda, who is sitting at the counter at The Ruby, the total showing on the front of The Ruby's cash register reads $4.75 but reads $0.46 on the other side.

REALITY CHECK

For a pro like Eric Peterson, taking his clothes off for Oscar's "nude" scene was no big deal. "At my age, who cares?" says Eric. "You can always count on the crew for a laugh."

QUIPS AND QUOTES

Oscar (griping about the sugar bowl): "Why didn't you put the lid on?"

Emma: "I never put the lid on."

Oscar: "That's what I'm saying … Thirty-five years we've been married and I'm always putting the lid on it."

Emma: "I wish you would put a lid on it."

•

Oscar: "I'm improving the room."

Emma: "How? By leaving it?"

•

Wanda: "I'm an enigma."

Brent: "Does that pay well?"

•

Wanda: "Do you like amethyst?"

Hank: "Yeah, you bet. Is she a wrestler or a stripper?"

Season 2
Episode 7

First aired: **November 16, 2004**

Writers: **Brent Butt and Andrew Carr**

Director: **David Storey**

Hero Sandwich

POPULARITY HAS A DOWNSIDE when Lacey invents a new sandwich that becomes a runaway success. The mayor of Dog River decides it's time to install a traffic light because of an increase in traffic downtown, but it comes at a price, and he puts pressure on Karen and Davis to bust jaywalkers to raise funds. Hank and Oscar turn into rebels with a cause, while Wanda turns to Emma for help in designing a tattoo.

16

Moose Jaw artist Johann Wessels created the painting of the squirrel holding a hockey stick, done by Emma for Wanda in the show. Johann, an acclaimed artist, found it difficult to deliberately create bad art.

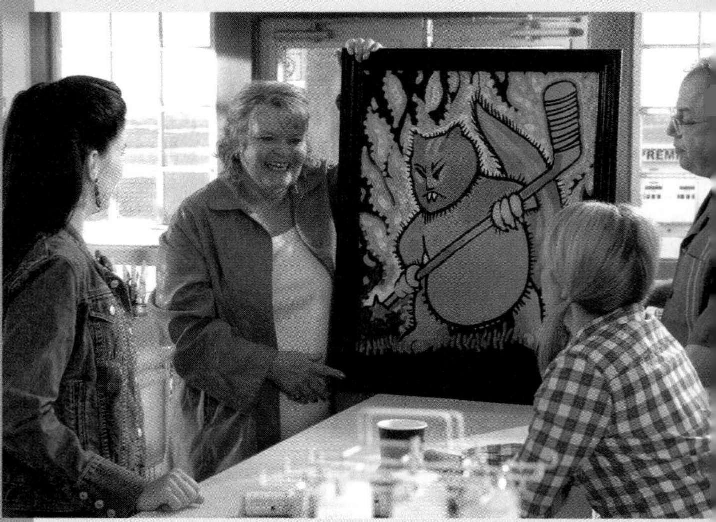

Art ache: Emma's painting captivates Lacey, Wanda, and Brent.

QUIPS AND QUOTES

Mayor Fitzgerald: "It's time that Dog River joined the 20th century."

Karen: "Now we'll only be one century behind."

HOWLER HIGHLIGHTS

- Crosswalk Hell: Mayor Insane
- Cattle Killed by Werewolfs

REALITY CHECK

The cover of the tattoo magazine that Wanda is reading in the store features a photo of an inked Crystal Waddell-Gardiner, the show's art department coordinator.

WATCH FOR IT

There's a camera shot taken through a (backless) freezer in Corner Gas. Guess who directed the episode?

Join the Infamous Ruby Club

Life in Dog River is not just about chili cheese dogs. In this episode, the town residents fall in love with Lacey's spin on a classic club sandwich. To tell the truth, quite a few Ruby Clubs, created by prop master Jay Robertson, were consumed during filming. The cast was keen to try one, all in the name of research, they claimed. Feel free to do some research of your own, courtesy of Jay's recipe:

3 slices of fresh focaccia (toasted, if desired)

mayonnaise

3 oz (90 grams) cracked-peppercorn shaved chicken, or similar deli-type meat

3 thin slices of aged Canadian cheddar

2 slices of tomato

2 slices of crispy fried bacon (optional)

salt and pepper to taste

- For the bottom layer, spread mayonnaise on one slice of focaccia, then add chicken. Place another slice of focaccia on top. Create a second layer with the cheddar cheese, tomato, and bacon. Season with salt and pepper to taste. Top with remaining slice of focaccia. Hold together with long, frill-topped toothpick. Serve with a sliced dill pickle, and french fries on the side.

Season 2
Episode 8

First aired: **November 23, 2004**
Writers: **Brent Butt and Mark Farrell**
Director: **Trent Carlson**

Security Cam

BRENT INSTALLS a security camera at Corner Gas to keep an eye on things but isn't prepared for what he captures on tape. Hank sees his chance to fulfill a lifelong dream to get zapped when Davis gets a TASER® gun. Meanwhile, Oscar and Emma's vacation at a fancy resort has them longing for home.

10

Check out the poster in Corner Gas for the Canadian Western Agribition, an annual Regina event.

Hot shot: Davis gets a new TASER gun.

QUIPS AND QUOTES

Hank: "I wanna be stunned."
Karen: "You're already there."

•

Brent: "No more dirty talk. Hand me that big tool so I can mount this."

•

Oscar (as Emma goes to put her head on his shoulder): "What are you trying to do? Head-butt me?"

•

Brent: "Wanda, can I show you something?"
Wanda: "I've already seen your belly doing the hula."

OOPS

When Davis zaps himself with the TASER gun, a bag of chips falls from the rack to the floor. In the next scene, it's gone.

COINCIDENTALLY

Brent Leroy says: "I'm not much of an actor really. I just play myself."

REALITY CHECK

- Wanda is often seen gnawing on red licorice. It's a favourite of Nancy Robertson's and a fresh supply is always on hand. "Sometimes it comes back to haunt me after a bunch of takes and I've gone through 10 long ropes," says Nancy. "I try to work it into scenes as often as possible."
- Lorne Cardinal (Davis) loved doing the physical comedy in this episode. "It was fun getting a riot shield in the ribs and shooting scenes with the TASER gun."

TOP PROP

It is a real TASER gun that Davis uses, but it was deactivated to prevent an accidental zapping. To be allowed by the manufacturer to feature the TASER gun, the show had to agree not to use the word as a verb.

- Oscar and Emma confirm that there really is love between the two by getting amorous on a road trip, leading to an on-camera encounter at Corner Gas.
- Director Trent Carlson wins a Leo Award for his direction of this episode.

Season 2
Episode 9

First aired: December 7, 2004
Writers: Brent Butt and Andrew Carr
Director: Robert de Lint

19

Bingo Night

WANDA IS A WINNER when she steps in as the town's bingo caller, much to the chagrin of Emma and her former streak of good luck. Lacey is puzzled to learn that the town prefers the chemically preserved "road cookies" that Brent sells over her home-baked versions. Hank looks to Davis to be his hangout partner after Brent starts spending more time with Karen, who has been temporarily suspended from the police force.

Call of the wild: Wanda fills in on bingo night.

Lucky charms: Emma plays her cards right every game.

ON A ROLE

Corner Gas fan Cindy Cherkowski won a walk-on role through a contest on the *Corner Gas* website. She appears in the bingo scenes.

REALITY CHECK

Some of the writers on *Corner Gas* are sci-fi fans, hence references to *Logan's Run* on this episode, and to *Battlestar Galactica*, *Star Wars*, and *Star Trek* throughout the series.

QUIPS AND QUOTES

Lacey: "Were your ears burning?"

Hank: "Ah, no, but I got a thing on my foot that gets itchy."

•

Lacey (referring to a package of cookies): "This is like eating a Bounce sheet."

Brent: "But a tasty Bounce sheet."

•

Emma: "Why don't you call [bingo]? You have such a beautiful voice."

Wanda: "But you threw your shoe at me on karaoke night."

Emma: "My feet were tired."

Season 2
Episode 10

First aired: **December 14, 2004**

Writers: **Mark Farrell and Paul Mather**

Director: **Trent Carlson**

12

Mosquito Time

HANK SEEMS STRANGELY unaffected by the mosquitoes that have invaded the town. Lacey finally feels like she's being included in Dog River activities when she is asked to contribute to the town's annual time capsule. When Wanda lures Oscar back to work for free at Corner Gas, Emma is puzzled by the peace and quiet his absence brings. Brent takes refuge at The Ruby, where he must endure Lacey's troublesome new self-serve coffee carafes.

Bug out: Mosquitoes show up uninvited for the town's annual time capsule event.

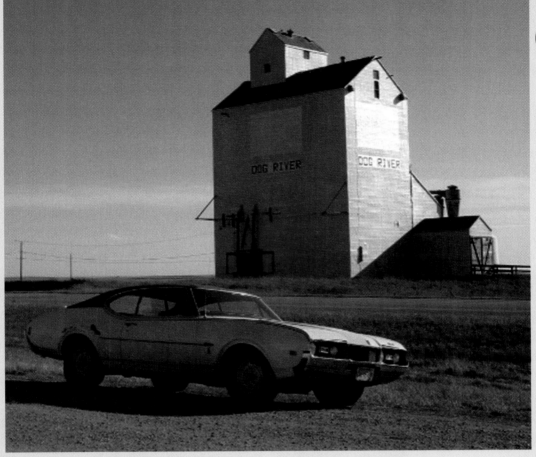

Hot wheels: Brent's banana-yellow 1968 Oldsmobile Cutlass is a true classic.

QUIPS AND QUOTES

Emma: "I need Oscar around the house. His insanity keeps me sane."

- Viewers get a glimpse at Hank's bathroom for the first time when he takes a bath—with his hat on.
- This episode marks the show's debut of the multi-screen shot, which shows four Dog Riverites applying dish soap to themselves in an effort to keep away bugs.

TOP PROP

The jigsaw puzzle is created from scratch, since one showing plenty of sky couldn't be found. Moose Jaw artist Johann Wessels painted the windmill scene and created the box top. His kids were paid to put the puzzle together. It was then taped together and broken into five chunks, one for each scene it was being used in.

TWISTED WORDS

"Liquid dish soap" to Oscar sounds like "lickey disco."

Season 2
Episode 11

First aired: **January 17, 2005**

Writers: **Brent Butt and Mark Farrell**

Director: **David Storey**

Guest stars: **Team Canada curlers Randy Ferbey and Dave Nedohin (as themselves)**

1

20

- The Clavet in Clavet Cup refers to a town in the province. The last names of the lead characters on the show are also the names of real places in Saskatchewan.
- The world's only curling museum can be found in Weyburn.

Hurry Hard

THE LEROY FAMILY has a long-standing tradition of being non-winners when it comes to curling. The town's tournament gives them a chance to prolong their dynasty. When a local senior's hip replacement creates an opening for a female team member, Lacey is in the spotlight as Dog River's most sought-after rookie. Meanwhile, Karen has been given the task of safeguarding the famed curling trophy—the Clavet Cup.

Ice capades: Wanda, Brent, Lacey, and Hank get swept up in the battle for the Clavet Cup.

REALITY CHECK

- Some fans who play in a women's curling league in Nelson, British Columbia, now yell, "Have a heart," in homage to Lacey.
- Writer Mark Farrell digs curling. Cast members Brent Butt and Eric Peterson have played too.
- This episode was shot at the Callie Curling Rink (Caledonian Curling Club) in Regina at the beginning of September. The production crew asked the rink to put in its ice a few weeks earlier than planned; the rink was kind enough to oblige.

Milestone

Corner Gas moves from Thursday to Monday nights.

TOP PROPS

Much of the equipment used in the episode came from a used-sporting-equipment store. The props department found a curling broom for Emma for twenty-five cents at a garage sale and made her a special curling rock out of Styrofoam.

QUIPS AND QUOTES

Oscar (talking about Myrtle, who was supposed to be on his curling team): "Good gravy! That woman is forever getting new hips. Soon as a new model comes out on the market, she's gotta have it."

•

Lacey: "Have a heart!"

Hank: "I think you mean, hurry hard!"

•

Wanda (commenting on Lacey's curling performance): "You did your best, Lacey, but you're no drug-addicted old woman who's had hip surgery."

STYLE ON FILE

- Oscar's vintage curling sweater, featuring a picture of a cowboy, came from used-clothing store Value Village.
- The Prairie Fire baseball hat, worn by Davis, belongs to Lorne Cardinal. The actor is a supporter of Regina's Prairie Fire rugby team, part of the Rugby Canada Super League.

Award winning: The coveted Clavet Cup sparked the competitive spirit in Emma, Mertyl (Gwen Seed), Oscar, and Davis.

Season 2
Episode 12

First aired: **January 24, 2005**
Writers: **Mark Farrell and Paul Mather**
Director: **David Storey**
Guest star: **Mark McKinney (as Bill from Wisconsin)**

JACKASS COUNT
1

COFFEE CUP COUNT

12

SASK WATCH

In 1976, the Saskatchewan Credit Union in Regina installed Canada's first ATM.

An American in Saskatchewan

BRENT STEPS IN as Dog River's goodwill ambassador when Hank is relieved of his duty after insulting a visiting American. There's peace and quiet in The Ruby when a new ATM at the liquor store draws a crowd. Meanwhile, Karen tries to learn French by immersing herself in the town's virtually non-existent francophone community.

Yankee doodle dandy: An American (Mark McKinney, left) gets a close-up look of Dog River, courtesy of Brent and Hank.

Border control: Bill from Wisconsin (Mark McKinney) takes a wrong turn and finds himself in Dog River.

ON A ROLE

- Ottawa-born Mark McKinney is the second member of *Kids in the Hall* to guest star on the show (Kevin McDonald appeared in Season 1's Tax Man).
- Mark Mallett is mentioned as being the former Dog River goodwill ambassador. The name belongs to a viewer who was runner-up in a contest on the *Corner Gas* website; runner-ups got to have their names mentioned in an episode.

REALITY CHECK

- In his office, director and executive producer David Storey keeps a vintage tabletop hockey game, much like the one Wanda and Lacey play at the beginning of the episode.
- Tara Spencer-Nairn (Karen) is bilingual, having attended a French-immersion high school.

QUIPS AND QUOTES

Mayor Fitzgerald: "My campaign to promote Dog River is working. An American has come here—accidentally."

TOP PROP

Finding a real car boot that could be locked onto the tire of Hank's truck to render it immobile was near impossible. The props department made one itself—out of a pot lid, a piece of vinyl fence posting, a lock, and yellow paint.

Season 2
Episode 13

First aired: **February 7, 2005**

Writers: **Paul Mather and Kevin White**

Director: **Jeff Beesley**

Guest stars: **Robert de Lint (as Hank's cousin)**

Pandora's Wine

OSCAR AND EMMA have their world turned upside down when Lacey brings a good bottle of wine to dinner at the Leroy home, and they have to say goodbye to their seven-dollar-a-bottle favourite. Meanwhile, Hank adjusts to his new life as a lottery winner, and Davis regrets listening to Karen, who pushed him into getting new shoes.

JACKASS COUNT

1

COFFEE CUP COUNT

7

SASK WATCH

As gifts to his pals, Hank gives them Harden & Huyse Belgian chocolates, made in Saskatoon.

Tight walk: Davis steps lightly in his new painful shoes.

QUIPS AND QUOTES

Brent: "It's my furniture of choice. The bed is the couch of the bedroom."

•

Lacey: "If I don't bring wine to this thing, what can I bring?"

Brent: "Low expectations."

•

Oscar: "You gotta stop living in the past."

Emma: "Does that mean we can finally get a digital clock?"

Oscar: "Sure, if you want to blow 800 bucks."

•

Brent (upon hearing that his parents want to invite Lacey over and get her hooked on Emma's hard-to-make biscuits as revenge for pushing them into more expensive wines): "Brunch is a powerful tool. I won't see it used for evil."

•

Hank: "Hey, Lacey, I'm still me. Same old Hank. I'm not suddenly Johnny Moneypants."

Wanda: "More like Johnny Grubbypants."

ON A ROLE

Director (Season 2's Bingo Night, and Lost and Found) and co-founder of Vérité Films Robert de Lint makes a cameo appearance as Hank's cousin.

REALITY CHECK

The storyline about getting bumped up into a new, more expensive wine bracket was based on a real-life incident that happened to writer Kevin White and his wife.

Clean finish: Emma's meatloaf wins a new fan in Lacey.

Season 2
Episode 14

First aired: **February 14, 2005**

Writers: **Mark Farrell and Paul Mather**

Director: **Jeff Beesley**

Guest star: **Aurora Browne (as Dr. Chris Garner)**

COFFEE CUP COUNT

13

Doc Small

LACEY FAILS in her efforts to convince a young doctor to set up practice in Dog River. Meanwhile, Hank becomes a man of no fixed address while his house is under repair. Brent discovers that there are plenty of hidden benefits to having only a $100 bill in his pocket.

Bad medicine: Lacey does her best to win over a new doctor for the town (guest star Aurora Browne).

QUIPS AND QUOTES

Oscar (about his houseguest, Hank): "I don't know if I like this ... some weirdo living in my home, taking up space."

Emma: "Welcome to my world."

•

Karen: "Lacey's talking to our new doctor."

Hank: "What's he like?"

Karen: "He's a she."

Hank: "The doctor is a transvestite?"

Karen: "No, Hank. She's a woman."

Hank: "She's a woman transvestite?"

•

Karen (posing a hypothetical problem to Hank): "There's a plane crash on the border of Alberta and Saskatchewan. Where do you bury the survivors? *Survivors* ..."

Hank: "Oh, survivors ... one on each side."

REALITY CHECK

Both Fred Ewanuick and Janet Wright are green thumbs when it comes to gardening. But in this episode, it's Hank who shows off his flora and fauna talents.

STYLE ON FILE

Take a good look at Brent Butt's glasses in this episode. They were custom-made, the lenses angling downward so that they don't reflect light during filming. According to director of photography Ken Krawczyk, the person responsible for making everyone and everything look wonderful in each scene, the crew tried everything during Season 1. They considered having Brent not wear glasses at all. They also tried special coatings on the lenses. In Season 1, you might notice that Brent kept his head down a fair bit. It wasn't because he was sad—it was because of the lighting problems. By Season 2, a solution was found, and Brent could finally hold his head high.

Sightseeing: Brent wears special glasses with angled lenses that won't reflect the camera lights.

Season 2
Episode 15

First aired: **February 21, 2005**

Writers: **Brent Butt and Chris Finn**

Director: **Wendy Hopkins**

Guest stars: **The Tragically Hip (as garage band), Jack Duffy (as Mr. Baker), Colin James (as guitarist at audition)**

Rock On!

BRENT, HANK, AND WANDA wax nostalgic about their old high school rock band, Thunderface. Meanwhile, Davis takes Oscar's claim seriously that Dewey McCloud, a famous singer, stole his song "Mona the Monkey." Lacey hopes to contribute to the community by uncovering the truth behind Dog River's name, for a town plaque.

1

11

Colin James, who guest stars in this episode, was born in Regina.

Rock talk: The cast was thrilled to have The Tragically Hip as guest stars on the show.

Greased lightning: Thunderface (Hank, Wanda, Karen, and Brent) rock steady at the Dog River Hotel.

REALITY CHECK

- At the beginning of the episode, Hank, Wanda, and Brent sing "Capital Cash" by a band named Fast Exit. The name came from the rock group that Brent Butt played with in high school.
- Tara Spencer-Nairn and Lorne Cardinal had no experience playing drums but received lessons before the audition scenes were shot. Nancy Robertson took up the bass guitar and quickly found her groove. "I was really playing it. It's one of my proudest moments," Nancy says, even though she developed blisters on her fingers and shoulder problems because the bass was so heavy. Brent needed no lessons. He has been playing guitar since he was a teen. Fred Ewanuick confesses, "I have no vocal talent as a rocker." Say it ain't so!
- The name of singer Dewey Macleod is a homage to two of Brent's friends: Dwayne "Dewey" Vogt and Garth Macleod.

Ratings spike to 1.9 million viewers.

ON A ROLE

Another of Brent's old pals, John Salamon, appears in the Thunderface audition sequence as "Large Man with Tuba."

WATCH FOR IT

"Capital Cash," sung by Thunderface, replaces "My Happy Place" as the song for the closing credits for this episode.

Dream on: Hank, Wanda, and Brent try on rock stardom.

STYLE ON FILE

- In a fantasy sequence, the members of Thunderface wonder about the life they might have had. Wanda is dressed as a pseudo-Madonna. She had so much hairspray in her hair that it took forever to wash out. "It was a good thing it wasn't grasshopper season," says Nancy. "They would have made a nest in my hair." A side-burned Brent dons a leather vest in an ensemble that could be described as BTO meets Spinal Tap. Hank's look pays homage to Mike Reno of Loverboy and the band's album *Get Lucky*. "I felt a bit bashful putting on those leather pants," admits Fred. "Everyone teased me. It was just an hour that I had to wear them, but it was an hour too long of my life."

- Brent's moustache and sideburns in the fantasy sequence were modelled after one of the crew—key grip Rob Parrell. Brent's instructions to makeup artist Krista Stevenson were, "Give me a set of Parrells."

Rock talk: The cast and crew were in awe of guest star Gord Downie and his Tragically Hip band mates.

TOP PROP

A particular set of very expensive drums had to be found for Johnny Fay, the drummer for The Tragically Hip. He has a contract that prohibits him from playing in public drums other than those made by Ayotte.

Twin set: Were Brent and key grip Rob Parrell separated at birth?

QUIPS AND QUOTES

Lacey: "That's a song? Sounds like a weasel caught in a chainsaw."

•

Brent (to The Tragically Hip): "Don't tell me what the poets are doing, just am-scray."

•

Oscar (about Thunderface): "What's all the racket? I can hear you clear across town!"

Brent: "You can hear us two blocks away?"

Season 2
Episode 16

First aired: **March 14, 2005**

Writers: **Paul Mather and Kevin White**

Director: **Wendy Hopkins**

Guest star: **Major Stuart McIntosh of the Snowbirds**

17

Air Show

LACEY CAN'T SEEM TO WIN when she tries to make it up to the people of Dog River for breaching air show protocol. She enlists the Snowbirds to help her make things right. Meanwhile, Corner Gas is closed for repairs, and Hank cleans up with his booming corn-stand business. To combat vandalism, Karen and Davis patrol the streets on bicycles.

Masters of disaster: Davis and Karen arrive too late to save Hank's corn stand.

QUIPS AND QUOTES

Brent: "What about a float?"

Hank: "It's a corn stand; there's not going to be a parade."

•

Brent (about Davis doing bicycle patrol): "If someone came after me wearing those shorts, I'd run too."

Wanda: "I might not."

•

Brent: "Hank, can I borrow some money?"

Hank: "Is that your official greeting now?"

Wanda: "Scorch! Pow!"

ON A ROLE

- Writer Paul Mather makes a cameo appearance as the gas inspector who tells Brent about a leak. Eventually, all of the writers appear on camera at some point in the series.
- This episode came about because the Snowbirds contacted the show and said they'd like to appear in an episode.

REALITY CHECK

- A man in the diner gives the raspberry, accompanied by a thumbs-down, to show his disapproval of Lacey keeping The Ruby open on the day of the air show. It's one of Brent Butt's favourite gestures of displeasure.
- Although Davis may have looked comfortable in his snug bike shorts, viewers didn't see the goose bumps on his legs. Filming took place during frigid weather.

TOP PROP

Props master Jay Robertson was the "chef" who created Kirk Berkley's Turkey Jerky, by drying shaved ham in the oven. He also designed its packaging.

WATCH FOR IT

Filming the Snowbirds in flight was tricky. The crew went to an air show to shoot them, but it was raining and the team couldn't fly. Although the next day was cloudy, the crew was able to get the shots needed. Post-production was an intense process of digitally cutting out from the film each airplane and placing it in the sky above the diner, to make it appear as though the Snowbirds flew over The Ruby. Jack Tunnicliffe and his talented gang at Java Post in Regina worked hard to get this effect to look believable.

Soaring with the Snowbirds

The Snowbirds

They might not officially be part of the diplomatic corps, but the Snowbirds have done a fantastic job serving as Canada's ambassadors to the world—much better than Brent or Hank did in that position in Season 2's An American in Saskatchewan. The Snowbirds came together in 1971 through the prompting of Colonel O.B. Philp, base commander of Canadian Forces Base Moose Jaw. Back then, they were an unofficial non-aerobatic team, their name a result of a contest held at the base elementary school. The team's first performance as the Snowbirds was on July 11, 1971. Over the years, they have thrilled crowds around the world with manoeuvres in their CT-114 Tutor jets. In 2005, not only did they make their acting debut on *Corner Gas* but the Snowbirds celebrated 35 years of flying high.

Season 2
Episode 17

First aired: **March 21, 2005**
Writers: **Brent Butt and Andrew Carr**
Director: **David Storey**

Slow Pitch

2

15

THE TOWN BECOMES DIVIDED by a supposedly friendly slo-pitch game in the local beer league. With his secret arsenal of pitches (including Hammer of Thor and Fried Green Tornado), Brent is ready to throw his way to victory. But it's up to Lacey to make sure the team doesn't get disqualified if she doesn't make it to the diamond in time. Meanwhile, Dog River's police force is happy to ignore the Dog River Guzzlers' drinking on the bench.

POPPED CULTURE

Wanda says that Emma has arms like Lou Ferrigno, the star of the TV series *The Incredible Hulk*.

REALITY CHECK

Gabrielle Miller loved the baseball scenes: "I kicked butt. When I was running and said, 'That was easy,' and I looked excited, I really was. I did hit the ball!"

WATCH FOR IT

The budget on this episode was stretched in order to rent a crane so that a shot could be taken of the Dog River Guzzlers looking upward at a ball that had been hit high into the air.

Cheer leaders: The Dog River baseball team having a ball.

Director David Storey wins a Canadian Comedy Award for this episode.

QUIPS AND QUOTES

Brent: "That's right, Wes is nuts. This coming from a guy who once punched a skunk."

Oscar: "He had it comin'!"

•

Oscar (reviewing the signals as third-base coach): "I rub my left elbow, bunt; I rub my right elbow, bursitis ... bunt ... bursitis."

Season 2

Episode 18

First aired: **March 28, 2005**

Writers: **Brent Butt and Mark Farrell**

Director: **David Storey**

Guest star: **Deanna Milligan (as Heather)**

1

6

Harvest Dance

LACEY WONDERS whether it's time to give up trying to fit in to Dog River after she discovers that she has not been invited to the Harvest Dance. Meanwhile, there's romance in the air when Hank scores a date for the event. But he and his new squeeze, Heather, may become star-crossed lovers after the town learns something unsavoury about her. Speaking of unsavoury, Oscar and Brent try every trick in the book to avoid eating Emma's jelly salad.

Two to tango: Hank and his date, Heather (Deanna Milligan), go out on the town to the Harvest Dance.

REALITY CHECK

- Gabrielle Miller and guest star Deanna Milligan have been close friends ever since they met at an audition when they were teens.
- Brent Butt has confessed a dislike for jelly salad: "It's ridiculous. It's horrible. Why are there carrots in my dessert?" However, his TV mom Janet Wright feels differently. "Personally, I love jelly salad," says Janet. "When I was growing up, my mom used to put cottage cheese in it, then the jelly on top, then flip it over once it set."
- In the final scenes of the episode, the cast and crew could barely contain their laughter when Brent hit the dance floor and was busting a move. "He really dances like that," said one witness who prefers to stay anonymous.

TOP PROP

The jelly salad was a special recipe created by the props department. Bananas, mini-marshmallows, fruit cocktail, and six packets of gelatin went into it. The result? A jelly salad so firm and rubbery that you could fling a baseball at it and it would still bounce back.

- The production crew is nominated for a Team Award from the Director's Guild of Canada for this episode.
- More than 1.9 million viewers watch this season finale.

Outside interests: Lacey and Heather share an understanding of being the odd gal out in town.

QUIPS AND QUOTES

Brent: "I heard Hank met a girl."

Wanda: "One that he doesn't have to blow up?"

•

Brent: "I can't eat your jelly salad this year, Mom. Lacey has me on some South Park Atkins Diet."

ON A ROLE

- Art director Dan Wright's daughter, Sydney, is the girl at the Harvest Dance who gives Lacey a bouquet of flowers.
- The band that plays at the dance was made up of all the drivers and transportation coordinators who work on *Corner Gas*. Casting them as such was the show's way of saying, "You guys rock!"

Season 3
Episode 1

Dress for Success

First aired: **September 19, 2005**
Writers: **Brent Butt and Andrew Carr**
Director: **David Storey**

WANDA UNLEASHES her feminine charms by wearing a skirt and makeup to work, causing Brent to wonder if she's got a screw loose. Meanwhile, Oscar and Hank take stock in imaginary investments to prove who has got tycoon potential. Lacey's attempts to thank Emma for helping her out at The Ruby when the dishwasher breaks down leads to a sticky situation that not even pie can fix.

3

12

A poster for Bohemian, a popular Saskatchewan lager beer brewed by Molson and sometimes just called "Boh," appears on the wall by the bar at the Dog River Hotel.

Chick chat: Karen, Wanda, and Lacey exchange gossip at The Ruby.

Skirting the issue: Chaos ensues when Wanda dresses up for work.

Animal Crackers

If you ever wanted to play a *Corner Gas* drinking game, you could do so one of two ways: Take a sip every time Lacey pours a cup of coffee, or take a sip at every animal-themed joke. Of the animals, the writers seem to favour badgers and monkeys (mentioned again in this episode). Funnily enough, the history of monkeys in Saskatchewan goes way back. Amédée Forget, the first lieutenant-governor of Saskatchewan (1901–10), had a pet spider monkey named Jocko. He kept a rocking horse in his study for it to play on.

QUIPS AND QUOTES

Wanda: "It's not a dress, Mr. Gucci. It's a skirt."

Brent: "Don't you think a skirt is a bit la-di-da for a gas station?"

Wanda: "I'm not the one wearing a powder-blue blouse."

Brent: "It's not a blouse."

•

Lacey: "Hi, Emma. I just stopped by to say sorry for before. And to make it up to you, I brought you a peace pie."

Emma: "A piece of pie?"

Lacey: "No, a peace pie—a pie to make peace."

Emma: "Well, thank you. I guess I did overreact a bit. Mmm, sure looks good."

Lacey (nodding): "Uh-huh."

Emma: "What?"

Lacey: "Oh, it's nothing. Well, it's just kind of interesting you'll accept this pie from me, which is $1.50 a piece, or $12 for the whole pie, but you wouldn't accept $20 for helping me with the dishes."

Emma: "Oh, I see, you're trying to make a point … this isn't a peace pie, it's a point pie. A patronizing point pie."

This episode has the highest ratings for a season premiere of *Corner Gas* to date, with 1.7 million viewers.

ON A ROLE

David Suzuki almost appeared as a guest star in this episode, but the timing didn't work out with his schedule.

REALITY CHECK

In one scene, Davis tries to scare Karen with a fake spider when she's looking for her hat. Originally, it was going to be a fake snake, but Tara Spencer-Nairn is so afraid of snakes—even fake ones—that she asked the writers to use a spider instead.

TRIVIAL LITTLE NOTHINGS

- The licence plate for one of Davis and Karen's police cars is 946 DYR.
- Wanda goes bare-foot in her sneakers when she dons a skirt.

TWISTED WORDS

- Brent coins the word *fakerupt*, defined by him as losing all of your fake money.
- Wanda comes up with "hormone-o-meter."

Season 3
Episode 2

First aired: **September 26, 2005**
Writers: **Brent Butt and Mark Farrell**
Director: **David Storey**

Key to the Future

1

5

WANDA AND BRENT do a little mind-bending with Hank after he becomes convinced that he possesses psychic powers. When one of his predictions for Wanda comes true, she's tempted to believe in his visions. Meanwhile, Lacey and Oscar team up to fix the town's pothole problem, and the police force learns not to forgive and forget when it comes to keys.

News worthy: Brent reads up on current events in the *Howler*.

QUIPS AND QUOTES

Hank: "I had a dream about your mom."

Brent: "You have five seconds to make my skin stop crawling."

HOWLER HIGHLIGHT

Hank Is Phycic

REALITY CHECK

- Gabrielle Miller can now add operating a jackhammer to her list of skills, as evidenced when Lacey tackles Dog River's pothole.
- Three key rings for Davis were tried out to find the one that was the funniest and fit his personality best. It's all in the details, they say.

She's got the power: Lacey hits the street to fix a pothole.

Season 3
Episode 3

Dog River Vice

Writers: **Brent Butt and Paul Mather**
Director: **Robert de Lint**
Guest star: **Ben Mulroney (as himself)**

EMMA AND BRENT go head to head in a battle of the vices. Emma tries to give up knitting, while Brent nixes coffee and struggles to cope in a world without caffeine. Oscar dives into Ukrainian culture with Emma, grateful for a new hobby, in tow. Hank takes full advantage of his new electronic organizer and the debut of a ride-along program launched by Davis and Karen.

1

21

Swing your partner: Oscar and Emma dance and twirl into Ukrainian culture.

REALITY CHECK

Emma and Janet both love knitting. "I hate waiting around, so it gives me something to do," says Janet. "Now it's evolved so that Emma always has a knitting or crocheting project on the go."

STYLE ON FILE

You'll notice that Emma is rarely without her handbag, even when she's Ukrainian dancing, a personality quirk that pays homage to Janet Wright's late mother. The Ukrainian dancing costume felt cumbersome on Janet though: "It had layers and layers. I don't know how they dance in it."

Gentle Ben: *Canadian Idol* host Ben Mulroney comes to the rescue in Dog River.

QUIPS AND QUOTES

Brent: "Quitting coffee is hard; quitting knitting is easy ... and fun to say. Quittin' knittin', quittin' knittin' ..."

•

Emma: "Why don't we do something un-Ukrainian for a change? Where's your clogs?"

Oscar: "Want to make *holubtsi* [Ukrainian for *cabbage rolls*]?"

Emma: "Not to you."

•

Brent (to Emma, who is trying to persuade him to cave in to his coffee addiction): "Don't push your stuff on me, Rico."

- Brent Butt and Paul Mather win a 2006 Canadian Screenwriters Award in the category of Best Comedy or Variety Writing for this episode.
- Viewers get a peak into Brent Leroy's bedroom for the first time.

Season 3
Episode 4

First aired: **October 10, 2005**

Writers: **Brent Butt and Kevin White**

Director: **Robert de Lint**

Will and Brent

OSCAR AND EMMA become suspicious of Brent when he encourages them to get a will. Brent does damage control—but not before his parents make sure Brent's inheritance is more punishment than reward. Meanwhile, the town takes a surprising shine to Karen and Davis's drinking-and-driving check stops, though Lacey's new bulletin board is enough to drive customers to drink.

Damage control: Emma, Brent, and Oscar laugh off a bike mishap in a fantasy sequence.

Tool time: Karen discovers a new toy with the purchase of a Breathalyzer.

Wanda refers to her son for the second time in the series.

WATCH FOR IT

A message on the bulletin board in The Ruby reads, "Will rake and mow anytime, call Danny W." Danny W. is actually the art director for the show. We hear he also does lovely landscaping.

QUIPS AND QUOTES

Wanda: "Hey, Lacey! I need your boards; I'm up to my armpits in bulletins!"

Brent: "That's almost two feet of bulletins."

•

Brent: "Am I a bad son?"

Wanda: "No. Mind you, my kid stuffs peanut butter up my nose while I'm asleep; maybe I'm not a good barometer."

POPPED CULTURE

Brent meets himself 20 years in the future in a fantasy sequence reminiscent of London Life's Freedom 55 television commercials. At the end of the sequence he screams, "Nooooooo!" just as Kevin did in *Home Alone*.

REALITY CHECK

Kevin White says that, in the scripts he writes, he works out things that have happened to him. That includes his parents spending a chunk of his inheritance on an elaborate, and expensive, paving job for their driveway.

Cheque mate: The children of Dog River are underwhelmed by Oscar's generosity.

Season 3
Episode 5

First aired: **October 17, 2005**

Writers: **Brent Butt and Mark Farrell**

Director: **Jeff Beesley**

The Littlest Yarbo

1

13

HANK IS SURE that the dog that found his sunglasses is actually TV's Littlest Hobo, the dog who comes to the rescue of those in need—like Hank. Meanwhile, Brent and Lacey can't seem to get it right when they try to order travel mugs for Corner Gas and The Ruby. Jealousy rears its head in Dog River when Davis and Karen get squeezed out of the do-gooder spotlight with the arrival of two firefighters in town.

Puppy love: Hank thinks he's found the Littlest Hobo.

Brent has a new nickname: "Corner G."

WATCH FOR IT

The usual closing credits song, "My Happy Place," is replaced with the theme from *The Littlest Hobo*, "Maybe Tomorrow," sung by Terry Bush.

POPPED CULTURE

Brent talks about Lacey doing a "Zen Vulcan mind twist"—an allusion to Spock, of *Star Trek*.

REALITY CHECK

The German shepherd featured in the original *The Littlest Hobo* series had salt-and-pepper colouring. The dog that appears in this *Corner Gas* episode is more of a golden shade.

TOP PROP

The steak that the dog grabs and runs away with is made of pliable rubber the consistency of thick gelatin. It was sprayed with canola oil to make it glisten. It was the dog trainer who suggested using a fake rather than real steak, saying: "I can get him to grab a real steak, but I won't ever be able to get it back."

QUIPS AND QUOTES

Oscar: "Some German shepherd came up and started barking at me!"

Hank: "See? It's the Hobo! This proves it!"

Wanda: "Sure it does. What other dog would think to use the Hobo's signature 'bark' sound?"

•

Brent (proposing going in with Lacey on coffee mugs): "I'll go halvsies with you. Pretty please?"

Lacey: "You know I can't resist you when you talk like a seven-year-old girl."

Brent: "You're the bestest."

•

Oscar (reading the logo on a travel mug): "The Rub?"

Emma: "What's that? A massage parlour?"

The Littlest Hobo was a bona fide international mega hit.

Dog Meet Dog World of *The Littlest Hobo*

Up there with hockey players and comedians, *The Littlest Hobo* is one of Canada's most beloved exports. The television show has two incarnations. First it ran on the CBC from 1963 to 1965, then, when CTV resurrected it in 1979, it became a syndicated hit around the world. Each week, a wandering German shepherd came to the rescue of someone in need, disappearing once his work was done. The dog of no fixed address was a true primetime superstar. The show attracted some illustrious talents, including then unknown Mike Myers (as the friend of a paraplegic Frisbee thrower), Rachel Blanchard (who later starred in *Clueless*), Patrick Macnee (of *The Avengers*), and Al Waxman, who directed an episode.

Season 3
Episode 6

First aired: **October 24, 2005**
Writers: **Brent Butt and Kevin White**
Director: **Jeff Beesley**

Mail Fraud

LACEY IS CONFUSED by the unorthodox way in which Brent takes his annual vacations and is determined to get to the bottom of why he never goes anywhere for them—even if it means intruding on his holiday. Meanwhile, a potluck causes Karen to go to extremes to ensure Davis does more than just bring napkins. Oscar surfs the interweb and causes alarm bells to ring down at cyberspace central.

1

11

Byte me: Emma helps Oscar after he stalls on the information superhighway.

QUIPS AND QUOTES

Oscar: "I put the gigabytes into the floppy drive."

•

Brent: "Yeah, it's my annual vacation. Comes around every two or three years."

Wanda: "Like my annual raise."

TOP PROP

Davis is spotted reading *Company's Coming Potluck Dishes*. It's a real cookbook, but at the time of filming it hadn't yet been printed and the publisher could provide only the book jacket, which was put onto an existing cookbook.

TWISTED WORDS

Brent coins the word *staycation*, meaning a vacation spent staying at home.

COINCIDENTALLY

Just prior to Oscar saying, "Commercial's over," the CTV network identification whistle can be heard in the background.

REALITY CHECK

- Tara Spencer-Nairn decorated her character Karen's fridge with real photos of Tara's close family and friends. Then she called them to say, "You're going to be on TV!"
- Janet Wright is a whiz on the computer. She even designs DVD covers for her movies.

Reflective moments: Brent soaks up some sun while Lacey ponders interrupting his staycation.

STYLE ON FILE

Brent wears designer duds on his "vacation." The gold Hawaiian shirt with white flowers is by Bill Bass, purchased at the discount store Winners.

- A glimpse into Karen's kitchen is the first glimpse of her home life.
- Second mention of jelly salad (the first was in Season 2, Episode 18, Harvest Dance).

Season 3
Episode 7

Fun Run

First aired: **October 31, 2005**

Writers: **Mark Farrell and Kevin White**

Director: **David Storey**

Guest stars: **Jann Arden (as herself), the then prime minister Paul Martin (as himself)**

1

6

DOG RIVER is holding a 10K fun run. Lacey and Wanda train for the event by starting a running group. Brent and others join but aren't able to keep up the pace. Hank makes a career move and gets a job as a crossing guard. Meanwhile, Oscar discovers that there is a downside to scamming handicap plates for his car when everyone starts treating him differently.

Minority retort: Brent Leroy shares the screen with guest star and the then prime minister Paul Martin.

Personal politics: Brent Butt and the prime minister get ready for their close-ups with help from the crew.

POPPED CULTURE

Homage to *The Bugs Bunny/Road Runner Show*, with an animated sequence that labels Wanda as "Fastus Cashierus" and Lacey as "Slowus Coffeeshopownerus."

REALITY CHECK

Tara Spencer-Nairn is an avid runner. She could leave almost anyone in the dust, and not just on a dirt road. Gabrielle Miller and Nancy Robertson also run to keep in shape.

- This episode marks the first time a Canadian prime minister has appeared on a sitcom. (Current Prime Minister Stephen Harper makes a cameo appearance in Season 4.)
- The ratings for this episode are just shy of the 2-million-viewers mark.

ON A ROLE

- The day Jann Arden came to set, the production was hours behind schedule. Jann was a terrific sport about it all.
- The scenes with the then prime minister Paul Martin were filmed at Hotel Saskatchewan, in Regina. He was sent a script to review ahead of time—"To make sure we weren't going to have him kicking a puppy repeatedly," jokes Brent. "The prime minister wasn't too bad as an actor. He was genuinely curious about what was going on during filming—'What's this cable for?' he would ask."

QUIPS AND QUOTES

Hank: "You know, I've been thinkin'. I don't contribute to society."

Brent: "Sure you do. You're a morale booster. By contributing nothing, you make everyone else feel good about themselves."

Hank: "That's not good enough anymore ..."

•

Hank (talking about signing up to be a crossing guard): "I was inspired by Mr. Stephens. Everyone he helps across the streets looks up to him."

Karen: "That's because they're kids."

Season 3
Episode 8

First aired: **November 7, 2005**

Writers: **Brent Butt and Paul Mather**

Director: **Mark Farrell**

Guest star: **Shirley Douglas (as Peggy)**

Trees a Crowd

It's all-out war when Brent and Hank rediscover their old tree house, only to find that new kids have claimed ownership. Wanda escapes Davis's police custody by showing off Houdini-like moves. Oscar finds himself in an uncomfortable position: in the middle of a potential love triangle between Emma and Peggy, an old friend who shows up in Dog River with romance on her mind.

18

Guest star Shirley Douglas was born in Weyburn, Saskatchewan. Her father, Tommy, served as the province's long-serving premier, from 1944 to 1961.

Out on a limb: Brent and Hank take control of their old tree house.

POPPED CULTURE

Wanda references the 1980s cop show *Starsky & Hutch* when she says to Davis, sliding across the hood of the police car, "Nice work, Starsky."

WATCH FOR IT

Wanda nibbles on red licorice again.

The manly cup: In Dog River, real men drink coffee—a lot of it.

QUIPS AND QUOTES

Hank: "To defeat a child, you gotta think like a child."

Brent: "Well, you are uniquely qualified."

•

Davis: "Please? Do it again ... double or nothing!"

Wanda: "Double or nothing what? We're not betting anything."

Davis: "I thought it was just an expression."

•

Hank: "Money is power, Brent."

Brent: "Is this where you try to borrow some power off me?"

Hank: "No. [long pause] Can I borrow 20 bucks for an unrelated thing?"

Season 3
Episode 9

First aired: **November 14, 2005**

Writers: **Brent Butt and Mark Farrell**

Director: **Mark Farrell**

Guest star: **Ralph Goodale (as himself)**

Picture Perfect

Brent tires of his camera being the brunt of jokes, so he puts aside his old-fashioned one in favour of a high-tech model. Meanwhile, Dog River prepares for a trivia showdown at the hotel, and Oscar unleashes his wrath against innocent ceramic garden gnomes that look remarkably familiar.

8

The guest star, former federal minister of finance Ralph Goodale, was born in Wilcox, Saskatchewan.

Gnome sweet gnome: Oscar discovers he has a twin.

ON A ROLE

Another writer is on the loose in front of the cameras. Andrew Carr can be spotted as the driver of the yellow car.

COINCIDENTALLY

- The name of the Wanda-Hank-Lacey trivia team is Wahala, a word that means "trouble" in the West African language of Hausa, spoken in Nigeria, among other countries. Seems a fitting name, eh?
- The episode aired, along with Ralph Goodale's acting debut, the same day he presented the federal budget.

POPPED CULTURE

Brent alludes to *The Flintstones* when talking about how a photograph is created: "A bird carves it with his beak." *Flintstone* fans will recall that in those prehistoric times, birds made photos by chiselling images into stone with their beaks!

REALITY CHECK

Before taking on the role of Wanda, Nancy Robertson wasn't much of a crossword puzzle fan—unlike Wanda, who loves them. Now, in between takes, Nancy can be spotted looking pensive as she works out the puzzles. She's tapped into her inner wordsmith.

Word domination: Wanda has mastered the puzzling pursuit of crosswords.

QUIPS AND QUOTES

Oscar: "Why can't we have normal neighbours?"

Emma: "Because you always frighten them away."

STYLE ON FILE

Mr. Goodale could have done the typical political thing and appeared on the show in a suit and tie, but he was happy to dress in farmer gear, a nod to his past role as federal minister of agriculture, from 1993 to 1995. The logo on his hat pays homage to his home riding of Wascana.

TOP PROP

The faces of the Oscar and Emma look-alike garden gnomes were sculpted by Diane Shannon, wife of props master Jay Robertson. Brent Butt loved them so much that he commissioned look-alike gnomes for each of the cast members as gifts. The one that looks like Davis has a rolled up copy of *Cosmopolitan* magazine under its arm.

Farmhand: Guest star Ralph Goodale (right) meets up with Hank at The Ruby.

Season 3
Episode 10

First aired: **November 21, 2005**

Writers: **Mark Farrell and Paul Mather**

Director: **Robert de Lint**

Safety First

KAREN IS FULL OF GREAT IDEAS for a colouring book for kids about bicycle safety but lacks the necessary drawing and writing talent to create it. Tensions between artist (Brent) and creator (Karen) mount, and the safety program might be its biggest victim. Hank's world is turned upside down when he learns he's a Libra, not a Virgo as he had thought, causing him to rethink his life and pursue a career in accounting. Davis and Oscar get stuck on the rooftop of the Leroy home.

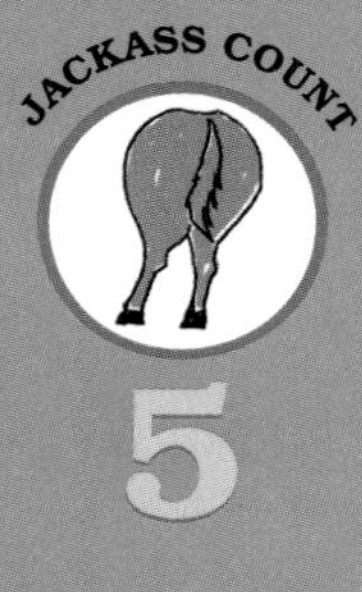

5

17

POPPED CULTURE

Brent says, "Throw me the idol, I'll throw you the whip,"—a line borrowed from *Raiders of the Lost Ark*.

REALITY CHECK

- Fred Ewanuick is neither a Libra nor a Virgo. His birthday is June 23, which makes him a Cancer.
- Writer Paul Mather *is* a Virgo. Another info nugget: His daughter is one of the children in the clown scene.

Hank goes hatless in public as he joins the corporate rat race as an accountant.

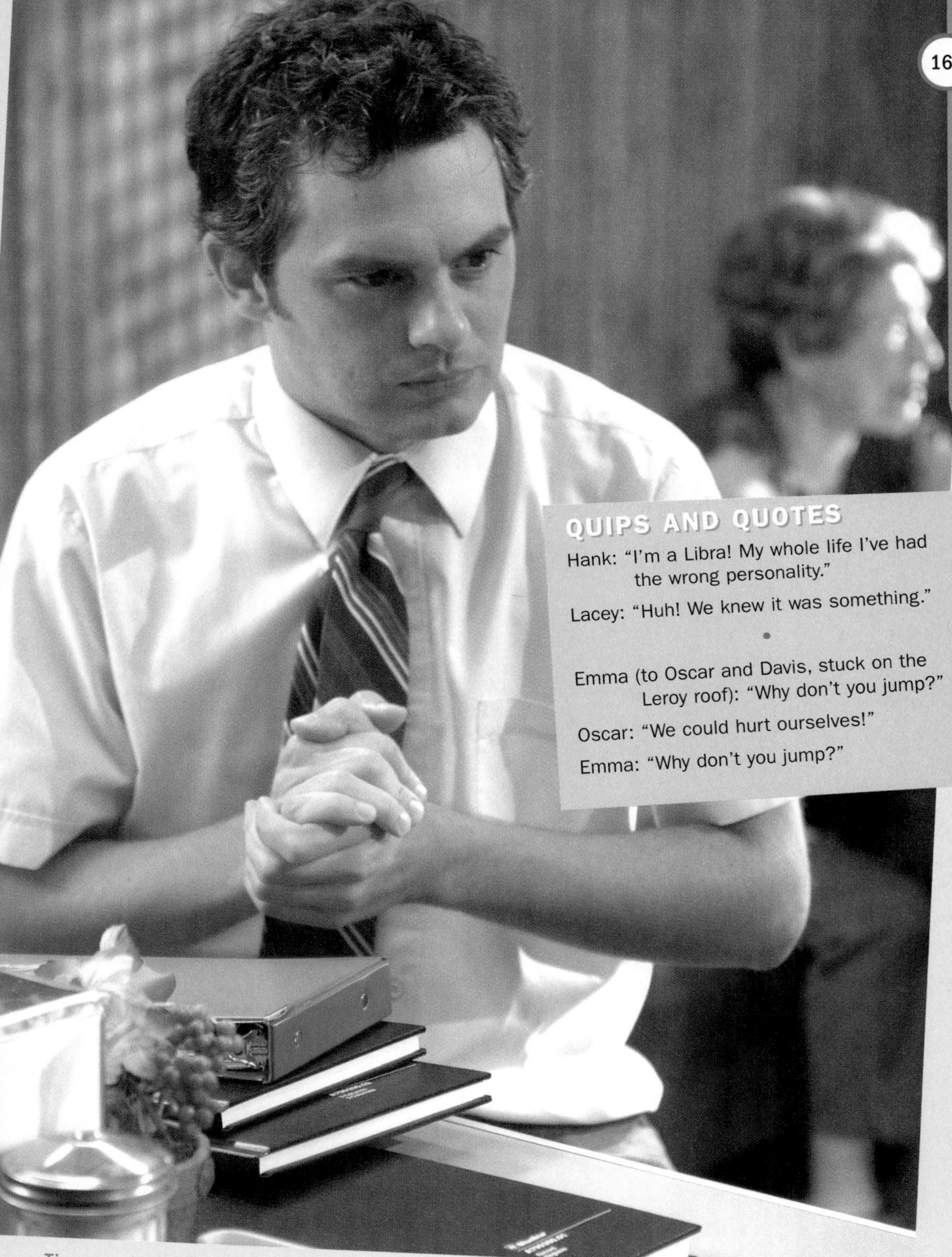

QUIPS AND QUOTES

Hank: "I'm a Libra! My whole life I've had the wrong personality."

Lacey: "Huh! We knew it was something."

•

Emma (to Oscar and Davis, stuck on the Leroy roof): "Why don't you jump?"

Oscar: "We could hurt ourselves!"

Emma: "Why don't you jump?"

Tie one on: Hank joins the corporate world as an accountant.

Season 3
Episode 11

First aired: **November 28, 2005**

Writers: **Brent Butt and Andrew Carr**

Director: **David Storey**

14

Hairloss

LACEY BECOMES MORE OF A HINDRANCE than a help when it comes to easing Brent's growing paranoia about his hair loss. Emma and Wanda square off over an ugly lamp purchased at an estate sale. Meanwhile, Oscar develops a childlike fascination of Lacey's so-called magic tricks. Hank learns that fixing appliances is a lot harder than hanging out at Corner Gas all day.

Bad lighting: An ugly lamp causes tension between Emma and Wanda, while Hank and Brent look on.

ON A ROLE

Corner Gas fan Berwyn Trapp, who won a walk-on role, makes an appearance, asking Brent, "Do you sell combs?"

COINCIDENTALLY

Lacey reads a book called *Magic Made Easy*, by Mark Mallett. The "author" was a runner-up in a story contest on the *Corner Gas* website. His name also makes an appearance in Season 2's An American in Saskatchewan as a result of Mark's first win as runner-up.

TOP PROP

Creating a lamp realistically hideous was a challenge for the props department. The lamp was assembled using parts from a statue of a monkey riding an elephant, and bits of an old lamp.

QUIPS AND QUOTES

Karen: "How did Florence die, anyway?"
Wanda: "Oh, ah ... she died of a rare condition called 'Almost 100.'"

•

Emma: "My elephant lamp! Where'd you get that?"
Wanda: "Florence Bickley gave it to me ... sold it to me."
Brent: "In Florence's defence, she was dead at the time."
Emma: "How could she sell you my lamp?"

•

Wanda (referring to the Roger Featherstone lamp): "The value of this stuff went through the roof when he went blind in 1903."
Hank: "I think he made this one in 1904."

Season 3
Episode 12

First aired: **December 5, 2005**

Writers: **Andrew Carr and Mark Farrell**

Director: **Robert de Lint**

Guest stars: **Saskatchewan premier Lorne Calvert (as himself), Vicki Gabereau (as herself)**

1

13

Ruby Newsday

LACEY JUMPS INTO the publishing business with a coffee shop newsletter. She asks Brent to draw the editorial cartoons, but not everyone in Dog River gets his humour. Always quick with a scheme, Hank counsels Lacey on how to make more money on tips at The Ruby. Meanwhile, Oscar goes after his childhood dream of being a paperboy, much to the chagrin of Emma.

Mugging for the camera: Brent joins talk show host guest star Vicki Gabereau for some java.

QUIPS AND QUOTES

Karen: "Humour isn't about making people happy, Brent."

•

Lacey (referring to her newly launched newsletter): "What do you think of the trivia section?"

Hank: "There's an air of triviality to it."

Lacey: "Makes you think, though. I mean Brent's cartoon is funny, but who knew that Saskatchewan was bigger than the entire country of Sweden?"

(cut to the Office of the Premier of Saskatchewan)

Lorne Calvert: "So what do you think of that, Sweden?"

•

Emma: "You're delivering papers? Wow, Oscar, I'm feeling something for you I've never felt before."

Oscar: "Pride?"

Emma: "Pity."

Paper ploy: Oscar comes out of retirement to begin a new career.

POPPED CULTURE

Writer Mark Farrell's obsession with *Buffy the Vampire Slayer* is evidenced by the tip jar question "Who's better at killing vampires—Blade or Buffy?" Hank then asks, "TV Buffy or movie Buffy?"

REALITY CHECK

Brent Butt is quick on the draw as a cartoonist. He studied animation briefly at Sheridan College in Toronto. He didn't finish the program but he did start a publishing company, Windwolf Graphics, and managed to produce two issues of the comic *Existing Earth*.

Saskatchewan premier Lorne Calvert makes his world acting debut, on *Corner Gas*.

Sask master: Premier Lorne Calvert takes a crack at acting.

Season 3
Episode 13

First aired: **December 12, 2005**

Writers: **Brent Butt, Mark Farrell, Paul Mather, and Kevin White**

Director: **David Storey**

Guest star: **Gavin Crawford (as Calgary airport clerk), Dan Redican (as Regina official)**

1

7

Merry Gasmas

BRENT ISN'T FEELING the holiday spirit when he learns that Emma is planning a traditional Christmas. Meanwhile, Hank is moved to organize a gift drive for a needy family, only to find them not so needy. Wanda is on the hunt for a Chewbot, the season's near-impossible-to-get toy. Lacey is heading home to Toronto, but poor weather causes a chain of events that ends with her not getting all that far from Dog River.

ON A ROLE

- Executive producer Virginia Thompson makes a cameo appearance as the customer who wrestles with Wanda for the last Chewbot in the store. "She totally nailed me," Virginia recalls.
- The Regina airport had multiple roles in this episode. It played itself in a stellar cameo but also doubled for the airports of Calgary and Edmonton.

COINCIDENTALLY

The last name of the "poor" family is Buckle, which also happens to be writer Mark Farrell's wife's maiden name.

STYLE ON FILE

Emma's Christmas sweater came from used-clothing store Value Village and cost $5. Janet Wright loved it and borrowed it for the holidays.

TOP PROP

The toy on every child's list in Dog River was the Chewbot. Created by Jay Robertson, this part-robot, part-goat combined parts of 10 toys. The goat head is from a farm play set, and the codpiece is actually a motorcycle seat. It took about five days to complete two Chewbot versions (one with the head on, and another with a broken head off). In his desk, Brent still keeps the anti-Chewbot—a goat with the head of a doll soldier, courtesy of the props department.

- *Corner Gas* films in Saskatchewan in the winter.
- This episode marks the first time the show has done a Christmas-themed episode.
- Ratings set new records, with almost 3 million Canadians watching Merry Gasmas.
- Congratulations to the cast for its Gemini Award nomination for Best Ensemble Performance, and to Mark Farrell, Brent Butt, Paul Mather, and Kevin White for Best Writing for this episode.

Fight club: Wanda battles a customer (a cameo by executive producer Virginia Thompson) for the last Chewbot.

Creative genius: Props master Jay Robertson and his infamous Chewbot.

REALITY CHECK

- CTV's Louise Clark and Brent Haynes had always kidded that they wanted the series to feature a goat and a robot at some point. In their honour, Chewbot, which fulfilled both of their wishes, was born. As Christmas gifts, the executive producers of the show gave Louise and Brent the original Chewbots. Today, the two Chewbots live apart—one in Brent's office in Toronto, the other happily grazing in Vancouver with Louise.
- Although it was wintertime, there wasn't enough snow in Rouleau for this Christmas episode, so snowmaking machines had to be brought in.
- According to line producer Mark Reid, who monitors where the moolah goes, the Christmas episode was one of the most expensive episodes for *Corner Gas*.

QUIPS AND QUOTES

Wanda (to customer, trying to grab the Chewbot): "Back off or you'll be sucking your Christmas turkey through a tube!"

•

Lacey: "Thomas Wolf said, 'You can never go home again.'"

Brent: "Who's that? Some guy at the airport?"

'Tis the season: The cast celebrates the holiday Dog River style

Season 3
Episode 14

First aired: **January 30, 2006**

Writers: **Mark Farrell and Paul Mather**

Director: **David Storey**

Guest star: **Amy Price Francis (as Connie)**

1

18

Friend of a Friend

LACEY'S BIG-CITY FRIEND CONNIE pays a visit to Dog River, but the townsfolk aren't impressed by her rude manner. When Lacey is alerted of her pal's poor behaviour, she's skeptical, thinking that the town views any non–Dog Riverite with suspicion. Hank enlists help from his buddies to pull off a covert operation that will prove to Lacey that her friend is nasty to the core. Meanwhile, a rewards card program launched by Wanda and Brent at Corner Gas is causing rivalry among its patrons as to whose business is the most valued. Karen takes offence at Davis's suggestions that she would make a poor undercover cop.

Rude awakening: Lacey sticks by her big-city friend (guest star Amy Price Francis), even though she has alienated the town.

POPPED CULTURE

- Referring to a zealous Wanda with her hand up in the air, Brent says, "I think Horshack wants to do it," —a reference to *Welcome Back, Kotter*.
- Connie, Lacey's rude friend, insults Davis by commenting on his size and calling him Ponch: "I thought *CHiPs* was cancelled."

STYLE ON FILE

Lacey's funky striped "lollipop" pants that Connie and Wanda make fun of at the end of the episode come from Gabrielle Miller's own closet.

TRIVIAL LITTLE NOTHING

What's missing from *Corner Gas* that is common in other comedies? There's no laugh track. As Brent explains it, "People are smart enough to know when to laugh."

QUIPS AND QUOTES

Davis: "You could never do undercover. You have to be able to act."

Karen: "I act like I get along with you, don't I?"

•

Hank: "Can I ask you for some advice?"

Emma: "Can't you ask your own mother?"

Hank: "You know my mom's gone on to a better place."

Emma: "They have phones in Saskatoon."

•

Hank: "You know what I hate?"

Brent: "When people just out of the blue say, 'Know what I hate?'"

Hank: "No, but that is annoying."

Season 3
Episode 15

First aired: **February 20, 2006**
Writers: **Paul Mather and Kevin White**
Director: **David Storey**

1

12

Filming for this episode coincided with celebrations held in Saskatchewan for its own centennial.

Block Party

DOG RIVER is celebrating its 100th birthday and Hank has big plans to mark the occasion—with a scale model of the town made out of LEGO® blocks. A building crisis hits when Hank runs out of blocks and is forced to get creative. The townsfolk have a good laugh at Karen's expense when they learn the obscure sport she excelled in. Wanda is a victim of her own success after she doth protest too much about holding any kind of celebration for her birthday.

Block heads: Hank and Brent build a replica of Dog River to celebrate its 100th anniversary.

A trip inside the real world of Hank with a glimpse at his bedroom and living room.

QUIPS AND QUOTES

Hank: "All great artists overcome adversity."

Brent: "Actually, most of them go nuts. Lop off an ear or two."

•

Hank: "I'll become a laughing stock."

Brent: "Yeah, 'become.' When have you ever been any other kind of a stock?"

•

Brent (upset that his mom gave Hank his LEGO blocks): "You can't just give away my old toys."

Emma: "Oh, you haven't played with those in months."

HOWLER HIGHLIGHTS

- Town Party Draws Celebs
- Horseshoe Champ Busted in Drug Scandal

ON A ROLE

In keeping with tradition, another writer hits the screen. In the flashback sequences, Kevin White plays Harold Main, the proud founder of Dog River's Main Street. White's wife, with their three kids in a carriage, are in the background.

REALITY CHECK

- As a kid, Fred Ewanuick loved playing with LEGO blocks. "I had buckets and buckets of them. I'd build cars, dinosaurs, and little towns."
- The writers don't have anything personal against rhythmic gymnastics—the sport Karen excelled in. Explains Kevin White, "We just make fun of things for no good reason."

Well built: The set dec team, consisting of Mark Dudiak (second assistant art director, Season 3), Daniel McKay (stand-by carpenter), Crystal Waddell-Gardiner (art department coordinator), Jay Robertson (props master), and Hugh Shankland (production designer), were the creators of Dog River in LEGO blocks.

TOP PROP

Upon getting the script for this episode, art department coordinator Crystal Waddell-Gardiner contacted the LEGO block people to get clearance to use the product on the show. The company generously sent oodles of free boxes of LEGO blocks to use. Hiring professional LEGO block brick artists (yes, there is such a thing) was too expensive, so the art department (Crystal, Mark Dudiak, and Shannon Berard-Gardiner) took on this huge project, which included building the exterior and interior of Corner Gas and The Ruby for the stop motion, animation-like sequence, as well as buildings on Dog River's Main Street, and the town's grain elevator. Jay Robertson built the LEGO block versions of Karen and Davis.

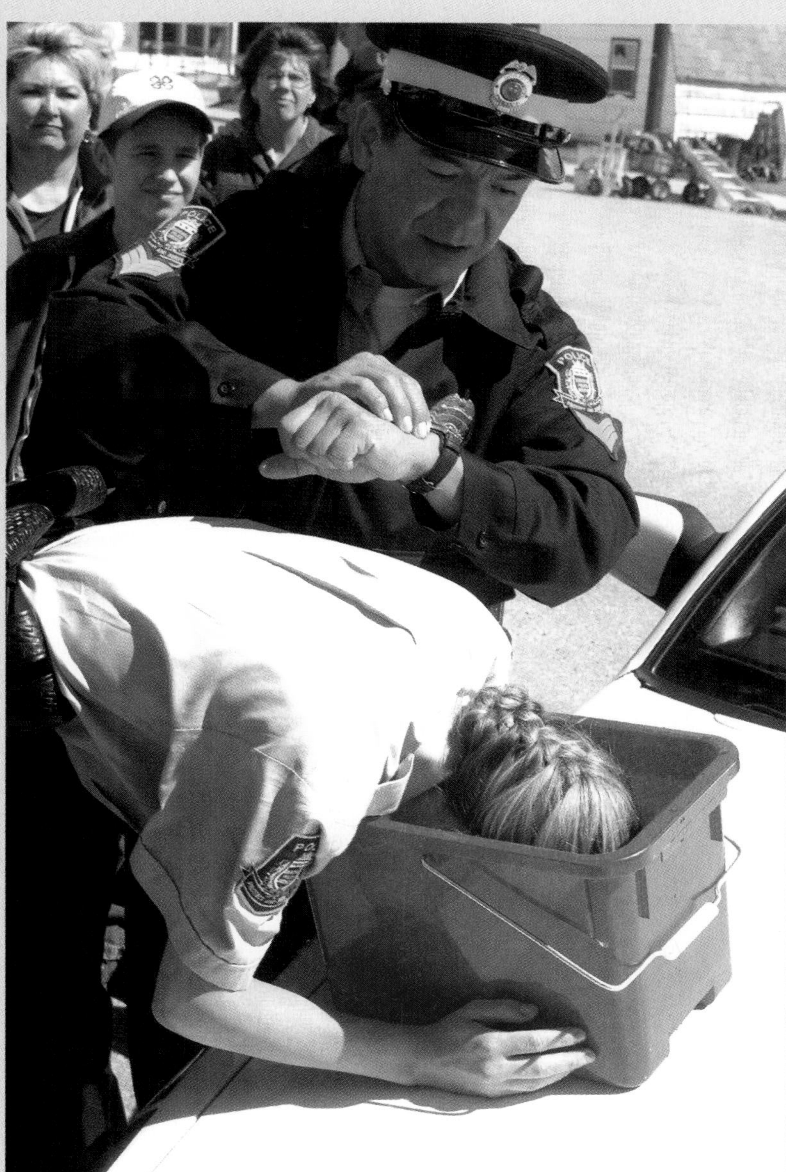

Taking the plunge: Karen's talents include holding her breath under water.

WATCH FOR IT

In the scenes where Karen demonstrates her unique ability to hold her breath, David Storey is given a chance to execute one of his signature shots. The camera was placed at the bottom of a bucket and a glass tank filled with water was then placed on top of it. The shot through the water captured Karen looking in at the camera from above. During the shooting of this scene, the then minister of Canadian heritage Liza Frulla was on set, and David invited her to watch the taping of this elaborate shot. Just before the shoot, the water tank inside the bucket broke, dumping water all over expensive camera equipment. Fortunately, the money to repair it did not come out of David's paycheque for that week.

Season 3
Episode 16

First aired: **February 27, 2006**

Writers: **Mark Farrell and Paul Mather**

Director: **Jeff Beesley**

Guest star: **Ken Read (as himself)**

1

17

In 1972, Saskatoon became the pilot community for the federally funded program ParticipACTION, which promoted fitness. In this episode, Oscar and Davis work out to the song created for ParticipACTION's Don't Just Think About It—Do It! campaign. The catchy ditty was featured in TV and radio spots from 1983 to 1984. The program was officially axed in 2001.

Physical Credit

BRENT AND LACEY are each out to prove they can keep a secret the best, while Karen is stuck in the middle of the battle. Wanda is confused when she learns that Hank was approved for the very same credit card that turned her down. Oscar gets physical, attempting to whip Davis into shape using tried-and-true fitness techniques.

Tee time: Davis and Oscar hit the links for a bit of exercise.

HOWLER HIGHLIGHT

Hank Gets Credit Card

ON A ROLE

Writer Paul Mather makes another on-camera appearance, this time as Frank, a customer at The Ruby. When Lacey blabs to Brent that Frank had to sell his farm, Frank overhears the conversation and sarcastically says, "Thanks a lot, Lacey."

TOP PROPS

- Davis reads *The Hardy Boys: Secret of Skull Mountain*. Originally, the idea was to have him reading *Lord of the Rings* or a Harry Potter novel, but clearance couldn't be secured in time for filming.
- The props department had to create a credit card from scratch since it couldn't get approval from any company to use its credit cards, as the script called for the card to be cut up. To make an original card was a labour-intensive job. Individual letters from a dozen assorted credit cards were cut out one by one and glued onto a blank card to spell out Hank's name. This was necessary since the script had Hank saying, "Feel how bumpy my name is."

WATCH FOR IT

The sound mic dips into the top of the shot as Wanda says, "Production values aren't important."

QUIPS AND QUOTES

Lacey: "What's new?"

Brent: "Wanda's cranky."

Lacey: "What's new?"

Brent: "Good point."

•

Oscar (trying to get the award of excellence adopted by the Olympics committee): "The old Ken Read would've done it. The crazy Canuck Ken Read ..."

Ken Read: "Those days are gone. I'm not crazy anymore."

Oscar. "No. You're useless."

•

Brent: "Lacey says I'm not a good confidant."

Emma: "Did she tell you that in confidence?"

Brent: "Maybe ... oops. None of your business."

Martial smarts: Oscar teaches Davis some signatures moves.

Season 3
Episode 17

First aired: **March 6, 2006**
Writers: **Paul Mather and Kevin White**
Director: **Jeff Beesley**

Telescope Trouble

When the door at Corner Gas breaks, Brent hires the best in the business to fix it. When Brent tries to fine-tune the mechanisms, his fiddling leads to the wrath of a true professional. Meanwhile, Wanda looks to the stars for a meteor shower with her new telescope, and Oscar and Emma embark on their own staycation in Dog River, in their rented RV.

8

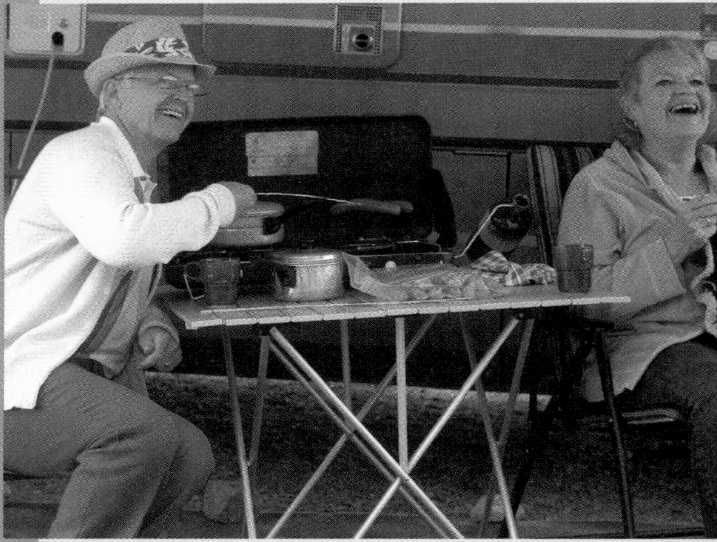

Camping it up: Emma and Oscar discover there's no place like home, even on vacation.

COINCIDENTALLY

The Prokopf meteor shower mentioned in this episode was named after writer Paul Mather's junior high classmate—"the type of guy who might just discover a meteor," says Paul. As a kid, Paul wanted to be an astronomer.

This episode features the only night shot of the series to date.

QUIPS AND QUOTES

Wanda: "Lacey, want to go to a meteor shower?"

Lacey: "Do I have to buy a present?"

•

Wanda (referring to Brent and Hank): "Hey, that looks like my telescope, except this one has two extra knobs."

•

Wanda (to Hank): "Why does the idea of a shower suddenly interest you?"

•

Hank: "I can't believe you're letting this guy fix your door for you. It takes away from your masculinity."

Brent: "You've taped every episode of the *Powerpuff Girls*."

Hank: "It's a good show. And I'm missing three episodes."

REALITY CHECK

- The french fries Brent is eating are real—and delightfully delicious. So good, in fact, that the cast often suggests fries might be a good thing to have in a particular scene.
- Wanda racing after Hank in the scene where he drops a television and breaks a bird bath and a car window was an unscripted moment.
- Don't be too impressed when you see characters carrying television sets: They *don't* have super-human strength. The inside of the TV has been gutted, and the glass removed and replaced with a thin, grey sheet of Plexiglas.

TOP PROP

It would have been easier to rent a telescope than make one, but the script required the telescope to go crashing through a car window—something the rental gods would surely frown upon. The props department made one out of tubing wrapped in vinyl, then glued toy telescope parts to it.

Eye spy: Wanda looks to the stars with her new telescope.

Season 3
Episode 18

First aired: March 13, 2006
Writers: Andrew Carr and Paul Mather
Director: Brent Butt

Bean There

BRENT SUGGESTS HOLDING a jellybean jar contest to raise funds to fix up Dog River's dilapidated children's playground. Davis takes a walk down memory lane by re-enacting some of his favourite moments from his most beloved cop-trucker movies when he sees a convoy of rigs pass through town. Wanda is a willing accomplice to Hank's plan to crash an event held exclusively for owners of Lamborghinis.

Taking the lead: Brent Butt slips into the director's chair for the first time.

Fast pass: The arrival of these Lamborghinis in Rouleau created a sensation.

TOP PROP

Where do you find nine Lamborghinis in the middle of rural Saskatchewan? Good question. First, Crystal Waddell-Gardiner obtained clearance to use the brand on the show from Alex Thompson, national sales director at Automobili Lamborghini in Toronto. He put Crystal in touch with Glen Kohut, president of the Lamborghini Club of Canada, who, coincidentally, lives in Regina. Glen linked up with Zahir Rana, who owns ZR Auto, a high-end used-car dealership in Calgary. Zahir helped line up a fleet of Lamborghinis and drivers. And that's how nine gorgeous Lamborghinis came to Dog River. It was quite the spectacle, ranking right up there with The Tragically Hip's arrival in town.

Brent Butt takes the helm as first-time director in this episode.

QUIPS AND QUOTES

Hank: "I could save up and buy a Lamborghini."

Wanda: "You have to save up to buy linguini."

•

Brent: "Look at that view. You can see for miles."

Lacey: "Yeah. Not much to see ... but you can see it for miles."

Season 3
Episode 19

First aired: March 20, 2006

Writers: Mark Farrell and Paul Mather

Director: David Storey

12

Road Worthy

LACEY'S QUEST for a new car has Brent lending her some of his "guy knowledge." Oscar's anniversary gift for Emma bombs, thanks to Wanda's well-meaning advice. Davis and Karen, meanwhile, try to curb their doughnut diet in favour of healthier but oh-so-less enticing options.

Shop talk: Brent helps steer Lacey in the right direction as she looks for a used car.

- The Season 3 finale beats the much-hyped return of *Prison Break* with ratings of 1.8 million viewers.
- *Corner Gas* remains the only scripted Canadian series in Canada's top 20 most-watched television programs.

REALITY CHECK

- Karen is reading a book by the name of *Uncle's Retreat*, by Elspeth Lawrence. The "author" was a runner-up in a cornergas.com story contest.
- The scenes of Lacey and Brent were shot very early in the morning on a gloomy day. The mood of the cast and crew brightened every time Brent said, "Is my bum getting warm?" In the end, everyone on set that day had fond memories of filming those scenes.

STYLE ON FILE

Although two green farmer's caps are available to Eric Peterson as Oscar, he wears the same one all the time. "I get superstitious," explains Eric. "I always want the one that has absorbed all the karma."

TOP PROP

The sign at the car dealer reads, "Storey-Thompson Motors," a shout-out to executive producers Virginia Thompson and David Storey.

TRIVIAL LITTLE NOTHING

This will be Lacey's third car in the series, but who's counting?

QUIPS AND QUOTES

Oscar: "I need a woman's advice."

Hank: "I can give you a woman's advice."

Oscar: "I'll go with a woman."

Hank: "That's sexist."

Dough nuts: Karen and Davis indulge their sweet tooths.

DOG RIVER
Windshield Centre
CORNER GAS

Fan Fare

Everyone is welcome in Dog River—that is, unless you are one of those radicals bent on filling in the pothole on Main Street, or changing the coffee carafes at The Ruby.

Corner Gas fans are a devoted, occasionally wacky, lot. They visit the *Corner Gas* website in droves, make doghouses that look like the grain elevator in Dog River, hold *Corner Gas* viewing parties on Monday nights, and travel from all across Canada and well beyond to see the Rouleau set. Even Hank takes off his hat to say thank you for your digging the show so much. You guys rock—harder than Thunderface, even at its peak.

Top 20 Burning Questions from Corner Gas Fans

INQUIRING MINDS want to know more about their favourite show, judging by the buckets of questions submitted to the cornergas.com website. Here are the answers to your most burning questions.

Where can I get a green cap like Oscar's?

You'll have to wrestle Oscar for it. The cap was custom-designed specifically for the character. It is not available to non–Dog River curmudgeons as of yet.

What does Hank do for a living?

Not much. If hanging around Corner Gas paid well, Hank would already be a millionaire (probably still driving the same beat-up old pickup truck and storing car parts in his bedroom). For a more definitive answer, let's ask Fred Ewanuick.

"Hank is a man of many trades," says Fred. "He's a travelling handyman—the kind of guy you call if you want a bunch of rotted lumber hauled out of your backyard for 30 bucks. He'll try his hand at almost anything, except maybe accounting again—that didn't work out so well."

Chilly reception: An episode of *Corner Gas* was shot in Rouleau during winter but snow was scarce.

Where's Wanda's son, Tanner?

Although the rumour circulating in Dog River is that Tanner has been sent off to military school in Switzerland, there's no truth to it. He's still around, since we saw Wanda battling over a Chewbot in Season 3's Merry Gasmas episode. He'll probably continue to stay in the background, which is likely safer, based on the spawn-of-Satan behaviour we saw in Season 1's Oh Baby. Nancy Robertson has her own thoughts about Tanner: "I like the fact that we haven't seen him. I hope we don't ever. I like the fact that viewers can create their own vision of him." Which may be an even scarier proposition.

How come Saskatchewan is never shown in the wintertime?

"As much as it would be fun, that would require shooting in the winter," explains Brent Butt. "The realistic reason is that in winter your chances of missing a day of shooting because of weather are greatly increased, versus in the summer. That would cost us $150,000 to $200,000 in lost time. Although we've got healthy budgets, we can't risk being dinged by those kinds of costs." Ironically, *Corner Gas* did make arrangements to shoot at the beginning of winter in Rouleau, Saskatchewan, for Season 3's Merry Gasmas episode, but there wasn't enough snow. The production had to get snow machines, snow blankets (to spread over surfaces to make them look like the white stuff), and fake icicles in order to turn Dog River into a winter wonderland.

Where can I find a copy of *Corner Gas*'s theme song?

The talented twosome, Craig Northey and Jesse Valenzuela, who penned the can't-get-it-out-of-your-head theme song, "Not a Lot Goin' On," released in spring 2006 a full-length CD that includes the single. *Northey Valenzuela* is available from True North Records, Canada's oldest indie label.

Why did Lacey say "YY-Zee" and not "YY-Zed" in the Merry Gasmas episode?

Man, did that ever get some folks twitapated. Over to Brent Butt to handle this hot potato.

"It makes me laugh when people get rankled over small things," says Brent. "The reality is that as Canadians, we sometimes say 'zee' and sometimes say 'zed.' It's reflective of us being culturally between the United States and Britain. We say it both ways. We're a nation of flexible people and we are very adaptive. That is what makes us Canadians."

David Storey points out that this scene was shot with Lacey using both pronunciations in different takes. The decision to use "Y-Y-Zee" was simply based on the fact that it was the take with the best performance.

Whose artwork appears in The Ruby—the painting that shows lots of clouds?

Saskatchewan artist Sara McCudden was the painter responsible for that piece, titled *Clouds by Craven.* Sure beats Emma's drawing of a squirrel with a hockey stick, huh? Sara also happened to serve as the set decorator on *Corner Gas* during the first and second seasons.

Where can I send a story idea for the show?

"Not to us," says Brent Butt. He's not being mean or unappreciative of your creative genius. It's just that for legal reasons the show can't accept them. Otherwise, lawyers and big books of copyright laws come into play, and things can become nastier than Oscar on a bad day. "The writers who we hire and pay good money for have good ideas for scripts, too. Since we're already paying for their ideas, we have to use them."

Can I be on the show?

"Yes," says Brent.

Where can I see the world's biggest hoe?

Plenty of fans have arrived in Rouleau to comb the area for the world's biggest, perhaps second biggest, hoe. The best place to see it is on your television set in Season 1's World's Biggest Thing episode. That's because the hoe never existed. For one scene, props master Jay Robertson created the handle out of special tubing, then had it painted to look like wood. The rest of the hoe was computer generated. The town of Rouleau has pondered the idea of actually building the world's biggest hoe, but there isn't anything happening on that front right now.

Why doesn't Hank ever take off his baseball cap?

Although it seems like his hat has been glued permanently to his head, Hank has been spotted without it a few times. In Season 3's Block Party, Hank grabs his

hat from the top of his bed's headboard before jumping out of bed to finish his LEGO block project for the Dog River centennial. He also forgoes his cap in favour of a shirt and tie when he leaps, briefly, into the corporate world as an inept accountant. In Hook, Line and Sinker (Season 1) and Mosquito Time (Season 2), there are also glimpses of Hank's noggin *sans* hat. As to why he's so attached to his cap, Fred Ewanuick has a theory: "Wearing the cap is easier than doing his hair in the morning. In Hank's opinion, someone who spends a lot of time on his hair is someone you should worry about."

If Davis lost his sense of smell as we saw in Smell of Freedom in Season 2, why did he say in Grad '68 that the bathroom smells great?

Yeah, that is kind of suspicious. In show biz circles, it's called a continuity error. In non–show-biz circles, it's an oops. But Mark Farrell, the supervising producer and co-writer (along with Paul Mather) of Season 1's Grad '68 episode offers a possible explanation (read "cover-up"): "At that time, Davis kept the fact that he was nasally challenged quiet for fear of recrimination. He said, 'The bathroom smells great' just so he could fit in with everyone else and keep his secret safe." If you buy that, I'll give you $20 from the money tree that grows behind the counter at Corner Gas.

How come it wasn't cold at the Grey Cup in Season 1's I Love Lacey episode? Everyone knows that it would be freezing that time of year in Regina.

Even a newbie to Saskatchewan like Lacey knows that, so why didn't the big brains at *Corner*

Does Emma really knit? Her projects seem to have grown by the end of each episode.

That Janet Wright is a crafty woman. She does know how to knit and crochet. But someone else does the knitting and crocheting that are seen in episodes of the show. In between scenes, actors are busy learning their lines, changing wardrobe, and practising their speeches for the Gemini Awards. Emma has some help off-screen to make her projects progress magically. Props master Jay Robertson's mother-in-law serves as a surrogate knitter-crocheter.

Gas? David Storey, executive producer and director of that episode, sets the record straight: "Those scenes were filmed in August on a day that was absolutely sweltering. The temperature was somewhere around 104 degrees Fahrenheit. The actors wore jackets and such, and they were melting under the heat. The scenes with Davis and Karen were just outside the gates of Taylor Field in Regina. Heat was radiating off the pavement around them. Not only did they have to say their lines, but they had to be funny as well."

There are strict labour laws in place that prohibit abusing actors by making them wears heavy parkas and wool clothing in temperatures over 100 degrees Fahrenheit. If this legislation seems unjust, please feel free to write your Member of Parliament and make a plea to have these laws repealed. Brent Butt adds, "For the record, there have been days of over 20 degrees Celsius [68 degrees Farenheit] as late as Christmas in Saskatchewan."

I would like to know which books were shown in the book club in Season 1's episode Comedy Night. I know there was *The Life of Pi* by Yann Martel, *One Hundred Years of Solitude* by Gabriel Garcia Márquez, and the last one had the word *saint* in it. Can you help me out?

The book that engrossed the members of the book club was *The Saint in New York,* by Singapore-born author Leslie Charteris. It was a particular favourite of the director and co-writer of that episode, Mark Farrell. He read the novel as a kid and it stuck in his brain. If you are a member of a film club, and not a book club, rent the 1938 movie of the same name that has Simon Templar (a.k.a. The Saint) taking on the New York mafia.

Is there a reason why Karen's police shirts are way too big for her? I think I must have missed an explanation somewhere along the way.

You did not blink and miss it. Karen's voluminous shirts have never been explained. But the inside scoop comes from costume designer Brenda Shenher: "In the first two seasons, this was the smallest police uniform shirt that we could find. For Season 3, we located one that was a bit smaller." By that time, though, Tara Spencer-Nairn had embraced the shirt's bigness and thought it worked as a character quirk.

Why do they spit whenever anyone says "Wullerton"?

Wullerton—*spit!* It's the God-given right of every Dog Riverite to furiously expel saliva whenever Wullerton—*spit!*—is mentioned. It's simply the way it has always been: a long-standing, totally irrational tradition that just carries on. Every town, big or small, has a rival. Just so happens that for Dog River, it's Wullerton. *Spit!*

In Season 1's episode Cousin Carl, can you tell me whether Cousin Carl is actually Brent Butt with a great makeup job?

A number of viewers believe that Brent was doing a double-dip in acting roles in that episode. It is actually Canadian comic Mike Wilmot who plays Brent's abrasive relative. Although he's not very well known in this country, Mike Wilmot is like the Brent Butt of stand-up comedy in both Australia and England.

Everyone knows that any self-respecting gas station in the Prairies sells diesel too. Why doesn't Corner Gas?

Brent Butt has two standard-issue answers to questions like this. It's either, "You just don't see it," or "Aliens did it." In this case, it really is a case of you-just-don't-see-it. The diesel pump is around the side of the gas station. For proof, here's a photo of the entire cast gathered around it that was featured on the cover of media kits sent out back in Season 1.

Wes man: Mike O'Brien plays the proprietor of Dog River's liquor/insurance store.

I love the show, but who's the actor who plays the guy with glasses running the liquor/insurance store?

The mystery man that you seek is Mike O'Brien. He plays Wes Humboldt. You might have spotted Mike on other TV shows, like the *Incredible Story Studio* or *renegadepress.com*. He's often cast as a dad or principal. Off-screen he does martial arts to keep fit and has his scuba diving licence—something that might come in handy one day in Dog River, or not.

From the Cyber Mail Bag

THERE'S A LOT OF ACTION at the *Corner Gas* website, cornergas.com, from playing the gas game to mayoral elections to juicy news about the show. It's also where fans converge to send their questions, thoughts, thanks, beefs, and griefs. A peak into the cyber mail bag yielded some pretty interesting stuff. Read on …

Good morning,

I am a master corporal posted with the National Support Element of Operation Archer. I am deployed to Kandahar, Afghanistan. I have been here since February of this year. I hope to be back with my family, friends, and colleagues of my unit (1 Service Battalion) sometime in September. I am sure the show's crew is aware of our deployment to Afghanistan. Further to say, quite aware of the rocket attacks we have been having since we arrived on ground. Well, I thought I should share this interesting little story I was part of …

About 21:30 hours, on 13 May 06, the camp was again under rocket attack from outside the wire. The sirens went off and I hightailed it to the nearest concrete shelter. The temperature at that time was a cool 36 degrees Celsius (temperatures have been hovering about 48 degrees Celsius lately). There were about 25 to 30 people hovering inside the shelter, waiting for the all-clear to sound off. One of these soldiers walked into the shelter, set up his chair, put a DVD player on his lap, inserted a disc, and started to watch a show. Of course, I was quite envious … I soon heard him laugh. My curiosity got the best of me and I gravitated over to where he was, and I was pleasantly surprised to see what he was watching. He was watching your show. It was the episode where the gang was doing interviews for a drummer and a guitarist for their band, with Tragically Hip and Colin James guest starring.

And you know what? For one hour, everybody in the shelter forgot there was a rocket attack happening (we watched another episode). We laughed and commented on the show's storyline. Before we realized what we were in the shelter for, the all-clear was given. I just wanted to let you know, your show made a difference to our morale for that hour. With all that is happening around here (rocket attacks on the camp, firefights, and ambushes on the Battle Group, ramp ceremonies for our fallen comrades), it is comforting to see familiar faces from home, laugh with them, and forget our troubles here. Even if it is for a short period of time. Thank you very much.

Ardis U. White, master corporal, Kandahar, Afghanistan

Thinking outside the blocks: *Corner Gas* fan Andre Lalonde of Saskatoon shows off his version of Dog River's famous landmark.

There has been quite a stir over this show *Corner Gas*. Been hearing about it at work, so I flipped it on one day and, wow, I was actually laughing! Hard! It was great. It is really nice that this show has a hometown feel and I can connect with it and the characters. I live in a small town, and it's like the same feeling here, the gossip and the diner chat. Awesome, I haven't experienced a show like this in a long time.

What's really nice is that this show is really becoming recognized and filling the homes of many Canadians every Monday evening. What's even better is talking about the show the next day. Humour, sarcasm, and wit—this show has it all. Keeps people interested and I feel good about watching it because it's not a U.S.–based show, it's from right here in Canada! Thank-you. For a true, downright funny show that warms the heart.

C.R., Keswick, Ontario

So I went to see the doctor sometime ago about a sore throat. As he is looking down my throat, he says to me, "You have a big uvula!" I say, "Well, thank you very much, but are you sure you don't say that to all your patients? By the way, what is a uvula?" He explains and I leave the doctor's office, all content about the fact that I've got a big uvula. But then I start wondering what purpose a uvula serves ... of all the people I've talked to, nobody can really say for sure. It's got to serve some useful purpose? Then I say to myself, "Hey, maybe *Corner Gas* is looking for a person with a big uvula. If they are, then my big uvula and I would finally have a purpose. So if *Corner Gas* is looking for a guy with a big uvula, search no further, I'm your man, give me a call.

G.M., Regina, Saskatchewan

The *Corner Gas* commercial, which introduced the first episode of Season 3, made me laugh every time I saw it. I love the part where Brent says he has cousins bigger than the electric car. For some reason that gets me every time I see it. Brent's dad is my favourite character. He's very much like a gentleman I used to work for, nutty but lovable.

C.D., Toronto, Ontario

Right on track: A railway through Dog River might look like this, in the mind of one fan.

I just started to watch your show after my uncle-in-law loaned me the first season's shows. I really love it. I would like to see more shows dealing with Wanda's demon child, Tanner. The episode where Brent babysat him and he had to call his mother helped me. I am starting to use that method on my two little monsters. Sometimes it works.

P.S. To Brent and Lacey: You both know that you like each other, so why not admit it and get married?

E.B., Kanata, Ontario

This is simply a note to the whole cast telling you what a great show you have. My husband and I are huge fans and hope your success continues for many seasons to come. I bought my husband Season 1 for Christmas, not ever having seen your show. I watched it with him and enjoyed many laughs. We are both former police officers (now in different careers), but get a huge laugh out of Dog River's only two law enforcement officers.

S.N., Keene, Ontario

Corner Gas is by far my favourite comedy show on television. I cannot tell you how much I look forward to watching Eric Peterson play the character of Oscar. I watch the reruns of *Street Legal*, another great Canadian show, and marvel at how the same actor who can play such an earnest Leon can also portray a cranky guy like Oscar. I did not realize or appreciate the fact Eric had such great comedic abilities. His delivery of his lines is hilarious, as is his character's body language. Janet Wright in her role as Emma is also one of my favourite characters. The interaction she has with Oscar is hilarious.

Corner Gas is one of those rare shows where every single cast member is amazing and important to the overall atmosphere, acceptance, and success of the show. For example, I cannot see any other actor playing the role of Hank. Don't laugh, but I think Brent Butt is a comedic genius for giving Canada and hopefully the world this made-for-television comedy gem.

Finally, I would like to thank the producers of *Corner Gas* for showcasing Saskatchewan (even though I was born in Manitoba) and Canada with the show and for not setting the show in a U.S. location or making the location non-specific like so many Canadian shows have done in the past.

Oh yeah, another thing: the writers of *Corner Gas* are certifiably disturbed—in a good way!

H.B., North Bay, Ontario

Franchise opportunity: A viewer found this Ruby's restaurant in Jamaica, but no chili cheese dogs.

I'm writing to you from Saudi Arabia. I had to write and tell you, first of all, that the show is incredibly genius and absolutely hilarious! I moved to Saudi two years ago and naturally the old homesick blues hit me once in a while. And then, one day, a Saudi man came to me and said, "Hey, aren't you are from that place called Sask-a-egina?" I said, "You mean, Regina, Saskatchewan." Turns out that we get the comedy channel in Saudi and the show airs every week. The show is a huge hit over here. When I was home this past Christmas, I bought the DVDs of Seasons 1 and 2 and brought them back with me. I have people coming up to me all the time and asking me about the show and this funny place called Dog River, Saskatchewan, asking me if it is really that flat there. My DVDs are continuously on loan to someone! Your show has been watched by people from Ireland, Thailand, Jordan, Iran, Philippines, New Zealand, Egypt, and the list goes on! It can be somewhat unnerving being in the Middle East at times so I want to thank you for providing myself and many others, here in Saudi, with a little bit of peace, comfort, and humour.

B.H., Riyadh, Kingdom of Saudi Arabia

Corner Gas has made it to Ukraine and has a small but devoted following here. My husband and I are originally from Saskatchewan but are now working in Kiev and have received DVDs of the first two seasons as gifts from family back home. There is not much English-language entertainment here, so we tend to pass around whatever we have. *Corner Gas* is a hit with friends from several countries (a couple have even ordered the DVDs for themselves and for family members). We love it because it is funny without being over-the-top goofy. We can relate to the characters and the situations on several levels, and there is no laugh track. Thanks for creating such a wonderful show and thanks to all the actors who do such a great job of portraying real people.

Wendy O., Kiev, Ukraine

I just wanted to drop a note to say thank you to the wonderful staff you have while filming in Rouleau, Saskatchewan. My son wanted to drive out there on summer holidays, so we did. It was just luck you were filming. One of the security guys gave us some commentary and was so helpful. I would also like you to pass on a very special thank you to Eric Peterson. We waved at him and he came over and spoke with us. He made my son's vacation one to remember. He was so caught up in the moment of talking with Eric that he didn't even think about asking for an autograph. Once again, to all the staff, thank you and keep up the good work.

T.F.-Z., Thunder Bay, Ontario

The summer of love: In June 2006, *Corner Gas* fans (left to right) Robin and Joni Tomlin renewed their vows and Betty and Gerald (Buck) Slessor tied the knot on set in Rouleau.

Congrats, we think your show is absolutely Canadian. Although we have Red Green and his famous duct tape, and we do enjoy watching him once in a while, we have found that we are watching your program, not once, but twice, and scary, we got all the jokes! My brother and his wife came to visit and gave us a wedding present. Guess what it was? Yes, it was Season 1 of *Corner Gas*. So you are thinking, nice but, so, and your point is? My husband and I have been married for 35 years and this is the first present he has ever given us. Now that is noteworthy! Anyway, we went to our son's place after Christmas and we introduced him and his wife to *Corner Gas*. Even better, we have something in common with our son—Canadian humour.

Thanks for being there and finding humour under the rocks.

C.L., Sudbury, Ontario

Supporting cast: To raise money for Regina's Globe Theatre, the stars of *Corner Gas* did a live performance of the Gemini Award–winning episode The Brent Effect, in front of an appreciative audience on June 17, 2006.

I just wanted to say how much I love your show. It's always funny and entertaining. It reminds me of my hometown of Wiarton, Ontario, every time I watch it. But the most amazing thing about your show is that it is the only show that my little boy watches. He is almost 21 months and the only other thing he watches on TV is commercials. He doesn't watch cartoons or any other TV show, but when *Corner Gas* comes on, he watches it for the whole half hour. I'm not sure what it means, but it is so cute that he likes your show. Just wanted to let you know.

D.T., Ayr, Ontario

On our last visit to Canada, by complete accident, we witnessed an episode of *Corner Gas*.

Very quirky. Our Canadian friends were kind enough to buy us the DVDs for the first season. However, we have now completed viewing that, and require an additional fix.

Why isn't *Corner Gas* played in the United States? Y'all weren't shy about sending us Céline Dion and William Shatner, who manage to ... hide in every possible corner of our collective psyche. If you Canadians would only send us more humoUr (we've been informed that Canadians really like adding the letter *u* to words) we 'mericans would be less likely to go out searching for weapons of mass distraction.

I hate to be adversarial about this issue, but if you don't get on the ball, we're gonna have to get mean. Yup, we're gonna send some of our most annoying talk show hosts and televangelists up there. I know that's mean, and hardly polite, but it just shows you how serious I am about this.

We need *Corner Gas* and we need it now.

L.R. and B.R., Munroe Falls, Ohio

I wanted to tell you how much I enjoy your show. It's very funny and well made. It should lay to rest the idea that Canada can't produce a good sitcom.... I do have one problem with the show, however. I find I am distracted by some of the actors' Hollywood teeth, which seem rather unlikely on rural Saskatchewanians. My suspension of disbelief is constantly shattered by those brilliantly white, perfectly straight chompers. They are what I call "Mike Bullard teeth." Last season, it was Brent. This season, it's Wanda. When Hank shows up with teeth like that, I fear I'll have to stop watching—unless perhaps you can work it into the plot somehow. Maybe the town is being taken over by alien pod people. It might work. Maybe you could get David Duchovny for a guest spot.

G.H., Muskoka, Ontario

First, my compliments on the show—it is witty, charming, and probably the most intelligent comedy on TV right now. The pilot episode could be a textbook for how to introduce characters succinctly and effectively!

I was eagerly anticipating the start of Season 2, and so was enjoying the first episode when I noticed something a bit disturbing—Tim Hortons coffee and Timbits in the police office. How is that possible? In the pilot, everyone sees Lacey as a "coffee saviour," and there is the further plotline where the price of coffee increases (what we refer to as the "Serpico" episode). And yet, here at the start of Season 2, Davis and Karen are supplied with Timmy's? It doesn't compute.

It really threw me for a loop—so I guess the question is, how far is Dog River from the nearest Tim Hortons, and is it within Davis and Karen's jurisdiction for patrol, or are they spending taxpayers' money to go afield for coffee? Someone tell Oscar—he pays their salaries! Sorry, got carried away there. Anyway, I love the show and hope it continues for a long, long time. But really, what's up with the coffee?

K.T., Kanata, Ontario (born in Saskatoon, raised in the Maritimes, now stuck in "Upper Canada")

What a great show, and what would it be without Oscar? The poor guy is so misunderstood! He tries so hard to please everyone that he becomes frustrated with the callousness of those around him. Even with his gentlemanly manner, he is ignored. He is always quiet, debonair, sauve, extremely modest, and never criticizes anyone despite the adverse comments directed at him. Oscar is truly a rich role model for the younger set, albeit lost to that ungrateful son of his. The poor guy never gets any respect and never gets a dinner, either. Oscar deserves a fan club and I would only be too glad to be a charter member. It's too bad that knighthood is no longer bestowed to gentlemen like Oscar anymore.

M.H., Calgary, Alberta

Glowing reviews: *Corner Gas* inspired one fan to carve out a niche for some creative talent.

In 1978, I had the privilege to [live] in Saskatchewan. My time in Saskatchewan holds a very special place in my heart. I was a mobility-impaired woman who found herself experiencing cultural shock in Saskatchewan. I was very green when it came to terms used by the folks [there]. I knew nothing about using north/south/east/west in directions. I really needed a translator when my church organist told me she lived five miles west past the swather and by the buffalo beans. I had no idea where I would end up. I had no idea what a swather and buffalo beans were! Was my face ever red to discover a swather was a piece of farm machinery and buffalo beans were a field of flowers. From the first time I saw Dog River, I felt I was home in Crane Valley!

L.L., St. Stephen, New Brunswick

Dear Oscar,

What have you got against rhythmic gymnastics? The sport takes a tremendous amount of hard work to achieve the balance and flexibility needed to perform the routines. Our senior girls practise two to three hours, five days a week to get ready for their competitions. Our motto is: "If rhythmic gymnastics were easy, it would be called hockey!" Any time you would like a demonstration, we would be more than happy to show you.

The girls from the Rhythmic Gymnastics Club, Saskatchewan

Absolutely love the show. I'm a Maritimer who married a man from Saskatchewan. So I love hearing his accent on TV for a change. Speaking of which, you could do a whole episode on whether or not *irregardless* is a word. I've never heard it used besides in Saskatchewan. Keep up the good work. My dad calls Brent the new King of Kensington. He says Al Waxman would be proud.

R.H., Dieppe, New Brunswick

I am a Saskatchewanian and I have been faithfully following every episode of *Corner Gas*. I love it. Very funny. I have made a discovery about the show's characters and wanted to let you know that I figured it out. All the characters' last names are Saskatchewan towns. How clever am I? Has anyone else made this discovery?

A.K., Yorkton, Saskatchewan

Elevated opinion: One fan gets crafty, with a re-creation of the Dog River grain elevator.

Just a quick note to let you know that both my husband and I watch *Corner Gas* faithfully each week. It's a great comedy that is sure to make us laugh and forget about any worries. I like to think of the show as the Newfie sitcom of the West. In case you're wondering, Newfie refers to Newfoundland and, yes, it is meant to be a compliment!

P.P., Fredericton, New Brunswick

Celebrity Fan Mail

CORNER GAS FANS are simply the best, as Tina Turner might say. Their dedication is phenomenal, astounding, outstanding, and stellar. The show also has followers among the celebrity set. Rumour is, George Clooney, Ellen DeGeneres, author W.P. Kinsella, and Cindy Williams (of *Laverne & Shirley*) are fans too. We asked some of the former guest stars of *Corner Gas* about their experiences hanging out with the folks of Dog River. Here's what they had to say.

Corner Gas is indeed a Canadian treasure. When I want my friends overseas (or even my American friends) to truly understand what it is like to be a Canadian, I send them Season 1 of the show. They often don't laugh until weeks later, when they realize that Canadians aren't really funny at all. Just weird and wonderful. My cameo was great because I got to run beside some really skinny little Canadian girls who made me feel like I had been eating most of Boston all my life. I liked being in the middle of nowhere in my retro white trailer, waiting to shoot my scenes. I thought I would have way more lines, but apparently, my dialogue was cut back due to … catering? I am hoping that someday the writers of *Corner Gas* will need a mute nun and that they will once again come to me, knowing that I have been acting for over four hours now and deserve the chance to win awards and walk the red carpet some day.

Jann Arden, singer

It is wonderful to see Canadians embrace a series the way they have with *Corner Gas*. It has really become symbolic of small-town Saskatchewan. A wonderful example of what Canadian television is capable of achieving.

Lloyd Robertson, anchor, CTV News

I don't want to say that I made the show, but my appearance in the first season pretty much saved it. The chemistry between me and Brent Butt was immediate. He's from Saskie. I'm from Saskie. He's funny. I'm not funny. Truth be told, we grew up about 45 minutes from each other (Tisdale and Porcupine Plain, Saskatchewan) and know a lot of the same people. I couldn't be happier for Brent. He's got *Corner Gas* and because it's seasonal work, he can still collect pogey.

Darren Dutchyshen, TSN

When we shot our segment, I had no idea what the show was about, nor did I even know who Brent Butt was. We all thought he had a great name so he must be funny. After having seen the show, I just love it. The cast is great. And so is the writing. I have had the pleasure to spend time with them and they are fantastic to be around.

Jake Gold,
Canadian Idol *judge*

Appearing in a cameo on *Corner Gas* was so much fun. The cast and crew were great. (It helps that most of them are self-proclaimed hockey fans.) The humour on *Corner Gas* is unique. It gets people involved, makes audiences laugh at themselves, while being warm and welcoming. It was a pleasure to be a part of the series.

Darryl Sittler, former Toronto Maple Leafs captain

My 28 seconds of screen time with Mr. Butt was the highlight of my dramatic life. The fact that it has been my only dramatic life is something I have to live with.

Vicki Gabereau, talk show host

My experience on *Corner Gas* marked my debut on a scripted comedy series, and frankly, I am surprised that I have not been asked back as a recurring character. I don't want to say I stole the show, but let's be honest. As my character said, "I am Ben Mulroney." I have spoken with Brent, and he promised that, if the show ever goes on location to Miami, Los Angeles, or a tanning salon, I will be the first guest star he calls.

Ben Mulroney, host of Canadian Idol *and* eTalk Daily

Appearing on the show? Well, given that I had no clue who Brent was at the time we shot that episode, I thought it was a sketch comedy program. Now I'm happy to have been part of such a smart show.

Zack Werner,
Canadian Idol *judge*

Now I see what all the fuss was about!

Sass Jordan,
Canadian Idol *judge*

I had never watched *Corner Gas* until my brother Cisco put me on to it. Then, when we guest-starred and I experienced the obvious brilliance of the cast first-hand, especially Gabrielle [Miller], I was totally sold. I wear my *Corner Gas* hat proudly every Saturday when I go to the flea market.

Farley Flex,
Canadian Idol *judge*

Meet Maggie Bertram, Dog River's Goodwill Ambassador

To visitors of the *Corner Gas* set in Rouleau, Saskatchewan, the face of Maggie Bertram is likely a familiar one. Although her official job is to provide on-site security, she also serves as an impromptu tour guide and goodwill ambassador for Dog River, meeting and greeting up to three hundred people a day who are anxious to know everything there is about *Corner Gas*. "Where's the surveillance bush?" she is asked at least six or seven times a day, or, "How come the cans of pasta are on the wrong shelf in the store?" "Can I get some gas and use the washroom?" is a common question, too. She politely answers inquiries, hands out postcards, and keeps the peace when fans come to town.

Her job working with *Corner Gas* started May 1, 2003, when a load of lumber was dumped in the middle of a hayfield in Rouleau. The wood was to be used to build the sets for The Ruby and the gas station. The production needed someone to babysit the pile of lumber. As construction got underway, townsfolk were curious about what was going on. Maggie, born and raised in Regina, was the one who filled them in about this new half-hour Canadian comedy that was going to be broadcast on CTV the next year.

Since the debut of *Corner Gas* in January 2004, the stream of traffic down dusty Highway 39 to Rouleau has turned into a sea of cars, buses, and loyal fans. Every day, rain or shine, winter or summer, they come to see what's going on and to get a glimpse of the sets that have become so familiar to so many people across Canada and around the world, from Australia to the Cayman Islands. The real excitement starts when the plywood covering the gas station comes down. In May this year, half of the kids from the local school were on hand to see the unveiling. Then it's time for the *Corner Gas* sign to be put up. "As soon as it's up, fans are on the internet letting each other know. Last year, someone drove overnight from Brandon, Manitoba, just to look at the sign," Maggie recalls.

There is a downside to Maggie's diplomatic role. If the show is not aired during its regular timeslot, Maggie's phone rings off the hook, with local residents wondering, why isn't *Corner Gas* on tonight? The other drawback is grocery shopping. Having appeared in the documentary *Beyond Corner Gas*, Maggie has become a bit of a celebrity. "I get recognized when I go to the Safeway in Moose Jaw. People follow me around the store and ask me all sorts of questions about the show. It takes a bit longer to get my shopping done, but I don't mind," she says. "I'm so pleased and proud to say that I work for *Corner Gas*."

Be Our Guest

DURING THE FIRST TWO SEASONS of *Corner Gas* so many fans came to visit the set in Rouleau, Saskatchewan, that Maggie Bertram started asking them to sign her guest book. In one week alone, a thousand *Corner Gas* aficionados had scribbled their names and left a comment or two. The United Nations would be proud to see the range of countries and cities represented in the pages of the Rouleau guest books: Scotland, Korea, Japan, Australia, Hong Kong, Phoenix, Brooklyn, New York, Kansas City, and Houston, to name just a few. Of course, Canadians, from British Columbia to Nunavut to Labrador and all points in between, dropped by to say howdy and more. Here are some notable comments, plucked from the thousands made by visitors to Dog River:

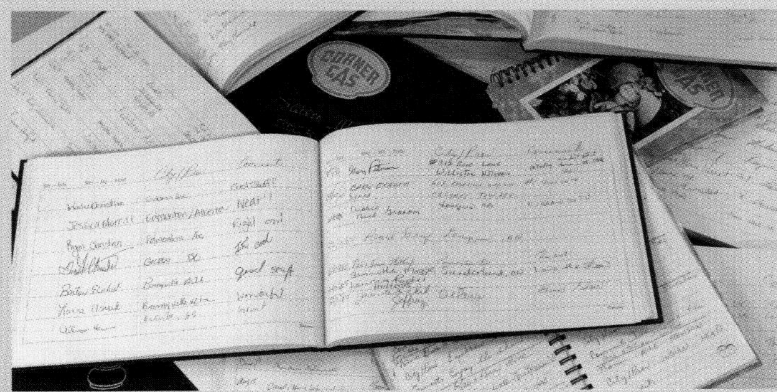

This is what makes Saskatchewan great.
K.M., Medicine Hat, Alberta

Look forward to seeing the show in Australia.
G.G., Melbourne, Australia

This is the second best day of my life, next to my wedding. It's the first, really, but if my wife sees this ...
S.S., Burlington, Ontario

Dog River?! I'm outta gas. Brent's big head is great.
A.Z., Burlington, Ontario

Love the Canadian humour. I will use parts of it to teach English in Chile.
J.A. and A.A., Guelph, Ontario (part-time in Santiago, Chile)

You have captured Saskatchewan's way of life. Too funny. Don't ever quit.
D.C. and J.C., Halbrite, Saskatchewan

Brent Butt's head is huge.
G.B., Medicine Hat, Alberta

Did you follow my dad around to get the perfect Oscar?
S.I., Red Deer, Alberta

I never dreamt that I would be in Dog River.
D.S., Ealonin, Saskatchewan

Did you call my mom re: green jelly salad? Scary how similar to my family.
Z.B. and S.B., Dorchester, Ontario

Best tourist site in the world.
P.O., Calgary, Alberta

Corner Gas is more than a show. It's a Prairie phenomenon.
A.D., Regina, Saskatchewan

Resource Guide

STILL WANT TO KNOW MORE about your favourite television comedy? Refer to this handy-dandy menu, chock full of resources that are sure to be as helpful as the wait staff at The Ruby, and then some.

More on the Show

www.cornergas.com

THIS AWARD-WINNING WEBSITE has been an integral part of the show since day one. Not only does it offer some great 411 on the show, it's also a fun place to stop, stay, and play for a while. Here's where you'll find a cornucopia of *Corner Gas* merchandise, from mugs and hats to DVDs and pins, and up-to-date news about the show. As well, it is home to the famous pump game, cool contests, and The Ruby Cafe discussion forum. Got something to say about the show? Drop a line to fanmail@cornergas.com. Or send your letter via snail mail to Corner Gas Fan Mail, Box 24037, Broad Street RPO, 2202 Broad Street, Regina, SK, S4P 4J8.

www.ctv.ca

THERE WOULD BE no *Corner Gas* without CTV. That's the plain and simple truth. Visit its website to find out what day and time *Corner Gas* is on in your neck of the woods. If you happen to miss an episode of *Corner Gas,* there's no need to fret. Last summer, CTV introduced Canada's first multichannel broadband service. Just click on the "TV On Demand" banner to find full-length episodes in enhanced resolution of *Corner Gas,* as well as other fave shows like *eTalk Daily, Canadian Idol, Degrassi: The Next Generation,* and even news. The sweetest perk? It's free. CTV.ca is also the place to get the scoop on the full lineup of shows on CTV, plus all of its specialty channels.

www.brentbutt.com

YOUR BEST resource for all things Brent is www.cornergas.com, but you'll find some good tidbits on his own website as well. Check out the audio clips (downloadable for free, by the way) featuring real comic gems from his stand-up routines. If you want to book Brent as a performer at your annual chili cheese dog convention or some such big event, you'll find the contact information for this here as well.

www.veritefilms.ca

BEHIND EVERY great show is a great production company. This website is the place to learn more about the evolution of Vérité Films and the shows it has brought to life, including *renegadepress.com* and *Incredible Story Studio*.

www.craignorthey.com

CRAIG'S THE GUY who sings the opening and closing songs on *Corner Gas*. He does actually sing other tunes as well. For concert dates, his bio, and his discography, this is the site to bookmark.

More on Places Connected to the Show

www.sasktourism.com

In the very first scene of the series, a Corner Gas customer said that there was nothing to see in Saskatchewan. He could not have been more wrong. Saskatchewan is one of Canada's best-kept secrets as a travel destination. Yes, there are lots of quirky big things along its highways, but it also has some of the best golf courses in Canada, great beaches (yes, there are!), yummy cuisine (saskatoon berry pie and Saskatchewan-style Nanaimo bars ... mmm), and cool sites like the RCMP Centennial Museum. It also has beautiful scenery, from unspoiled pine forests to sand dunes and waterfalls. Tourism Saskatchewan will gladly send you brochures and other information so that you can plan your trip to the province (call toll-free 1-877-237-2273).

---

www.townofrouleau.com

When you head to Saskatchewan, be sure to stop in at the real Dog River, the town of Rouleau. This is where the cast and crew come together to film parts of the show. Head to the centre of town to see the buildings used for many of the exterior shots in the series. The town's website provides the full scoop on what Rouleau has to offer.

More on *Corner Gas* Set Tours

www.cnttours.ca

Take a peak behind the magic of television and *Corner Gas*. This private company offers tours of the sets both in Rouleau and Regina for a few months each year. Tours depart from Regina.

Acknowledgments

PUTTING TOGETHER this book was a fun yet challenging project, but with the help I received from all directions, it came to fruition—the result of which you see before you.

A heartfelt *thank you* to all those who kept the book humming along nicely over the last year and a half, including my agent Robert Lecker; the dynamic duo from Vérité Films, Virginia Thompson and Sarah Fedorchuk; my hero Scott Henderson, from CTV; all the various lawyers involved; and, last but not least, the girl-powered editorial team at Penguin Group (Canada), Helen Reeves, Tracy Bordian, and Judy Phillips.

Buckets of gratitude to the cast and crew of *Corner Gas*. I appreciate you sharing your personal stories, insights, and gossip. Special thanks to Brent Butt, David Storey, Nancy

Robertson, Fred Ewanuick, Gabrielle Miller, Janet Wright, Eric Peterson, Lorne Cardinal, Tara Spencer-Nairn, Jay Robertson, Brenda Shenher, Mark Farrell, Paul Mather, Kevin White, Andrew Carr, Hugh Shankland, Mark Reid, Ken Krawczyk, Allan Feildel, Craig Northey, Sara Longfellow, Crystal Waddell-Gardiner, and Maggie Bertram. A thank you also to Rouleau mayor Kenneth Hoff and to Daryl Demoskoff from Tourism Saskatchewan for telling me what a biffie was, and other assistance. A giant *merci beaucoup* to the folks at CTV who were so generous with their time and support of this project: Susanne Boyce, Ed Robinson, Brent Haynes, Mike Cosentino, and Jim Quan.

Saskatchewan Trivia Challenge, by Robin and Arlene Karpan (Parkland Publishing), proved a great resource in my research for this book, while the booklet *A Record of Activities and Reminiscences of Rouleau and District: Saskatchewan Homecoming '71,* compiled by the Rouleau Historical Committee, gave me insight into the town.

Much love and special thanks with sugar on top goes to Catherine Garnier, my best friend, my muse, and so much more. I really could not have done it without you.

Michele Sponagle is a Toronto-based journalist and editor who has contributed to many of Canada's best-known publications, including *Flare, Chatelaine, enRoute, The Globe and Mail, Elm Street,* and *Canadian Living*. The Hamilton-born writer has covered a wide range of lifestyle topics, from travel to pop culture, from health to television. Throughout her career, she has interviewed a number of celebrities, Gwen Stefani, Evangeline Lilly, Susan Sarandon, and Teri Hatcher among them. Her writing has been nominated for a National Magazine Award and a Western Magazine Award.

Photo Credits

All photos are courtesy of Allan Feildel for CTV, with the following exceptions:

page 10: Rouleau mileage sign, Michele Sponagle

page 14: Dog River Hotel, Michele Sponagle

page 15: Rouleau post office, Michele Sponagle

page 19: catering truck, Michele Sponagle

pages 28–31: character shots, Kharen Hill for CTV

page 41: Craig Northey and Doug Elliott at Corner Gas Live!, Greg Henkenhaf for CTV

pages 46–47: Brent Butt at gas giveaway, Greg Henkenhaf for CTV

page 53: Brent Butt at Corner Gas Live!, Greg Henkenhaf for CTV

page 70: Davis Quinton, Kharen Hill for CTV

page 78: Brent and Oscar Leroy, Kharen Hill for CTV

page 90: world's largest honeybee, town of Tisdale, Saskatchewan

page 105: Taylor Field in Regina, Tourism Saskatchewan

page 125: Brent Leroy's car, Michele Sponagle

page 139: The Snowbirds, of Tourism Saskatchewan

page 145: Lieutenant-Governor Forget with his monkey Jocko, R-A7593, Saskatchewan Archives Board

page 201: Jann Arden, photographed by Andrew MacNaughtan, courtesy of Universal Music Canada

page 211: Welcome to Rouleau sign, Michele Sponagle

Illustrations on pages xi, 188, 194, courtesy of Alanna Cavanagh

Welcome to Rouleau
A.K.A.
"Dog River"
CORNER GAS
HOME OF "CORNER GAS"
CTV